POP ART

KRIS GALICIA BROWN

POP ART

DECORATING & SHAPING

custom cake *pops*

FRONT TABLE BOOKS
AN IMPRINT OF CEDAR FORT, INC.
SPRINGVILLE, UTAH

Cover photography by Kris Galicia Brown, except strawberry cake pops, by Melissa Biador Photography

ISBN 13: 978-1-4621-1258-6

Published by Front Table Books, an imprint of Cedar Fort, Inc.
2373 W. 700 S., Springville, UT 84663
Distributed by Cedar Fort, Inc., www.cedarfort.com

Library of Congress Cataloging-in-Publication Data on file

Cover and page design by Erica Dixon
Cover design © 2013 by Lyle Mortimer
Edited by Casey J. Winters

Printed in China

10 9 8 7 6 5 4 3 2 1

For my favorite sweets—London and Cali

Contents

CONTENTS

CAKE AND BINDER RECIPES 155

Cakes

Binders

CAKE AND CANDY SUPPLIES 163

INDEX 167 · ABOUT THE AUTHOR 171

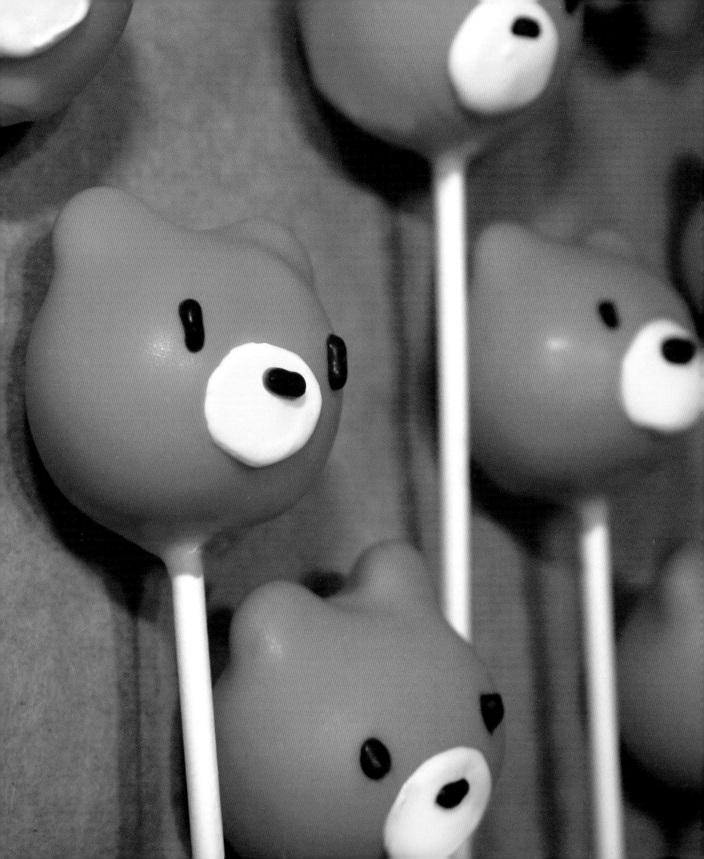

Acknowledgments

My husband, Pierre: I love you. Thank you for supporting me without question or hesitation in this crazy venture. You're the best number-one fan, motivator, and quality control department ever.

Mom: You are such a radiant light. Thank you for always encouraging my creativity and instilling my fearlessness to approach and take risks confidently.

My family and friends: Thank you for the daily encouragement and love and for providing a solid base that keeps me humbled, grounded, and smiling. I love you guys! Jessi and Rai, here you go.

Standlee's Team: Sandy, Cheryl, Jessica, Jose, and Caitlyn—thanks for the constant encouragement and opportunity to teach my craft at your store. And thank you for allowing me to be a part of your *Good Morning San Diego* TV feature.

Bobby Sim: The person behind my website and rebranding. You're a graphic design genius and a good friend. Thank you for all you've done. Much love.

My most amazing publishing team: You helped transform my cake pop knowledge into this beautiful book, I cannot thank you enough: Joanna, Matice, Erica, Casey, Alissa, and the entire Cedar Fort team.

Contributing photographers: Chris Wojdak Photography, Nicole Benitez Photography, Heart and Country, Melissa Biador Photography, Sonny and Jennifer Sbranti—thank you for capturing such stunning photos of me and my cake pops!

My fans: You are all the bottomless source of my inspiration. Thank you for your willingness to see what I come up with next. Thank you for joining me on this awesome journey!

Life is sweeeet!

"**ART** *is what* **you can GET AWAY** *with.*"

Andy Warhol

Introduction

I am so excited to share my love for cake pops with you and have them come to life in your kitchens! This book contains my personal methods, techniques, tips, and tricks to making awesome custom cake pops. Read each section carefully before diving into cake pop making. It's not a quick process, but when you plan ahead and take your time, the sense of accomplishment you feel is amazing. Most cake pop designs featured in this book have a stopping point for beginners as well as extra steps for the more advanced reader.

I am an artist. My background has nothing to do with baking but everything to do with design. I am not a formally trained pastry chef, but I am an overly zealous baker. I'm a graphic designer by trade but a sweets connoisseur at heart. I have a sweet tooth—probably more than one. I have a beyond-love for chocolate, and I have also been known to empty bakeries of snickerdoodle cookies. Stepping into the world of cake pops has brought me into the most creative arena of my life. I enjoy the challenge of piecing cake together with other candies and sweets to create tiny edible masterpieces, and I am excited to share my processes with you.

Integrating art into sweets is what I love doing. Much like the Pop Art movement in the 1950s emerging and presenting a challenge to traditional fine art, cake pops have taken the sweets industry by storm. It's a new concept, a new breed of goods that presents a challenge to classic and traditional pastries. Thank you for being a part of this sweet whirlwind! Get ready to make some of these small, beautiful, incredibly irresistible, and incredibly satisfying treats!

KRIS GALICIA BROWN

Tools and Equipment

I'm a big believer in that to fully enjoy a hobby, it must be easy to jump into. You'll find that most of the tools I've listed in this section are already in your kitchen or are easy and inexpensive to acquire.

The items listed in this section are what you'll need to create the custom cake pops in this book. Remember to plan ahead and set aside a few hours so you can take your time with making these sweet treats.

MY FAVORITE TOOLS

Silicone bowls (1-cup capacity): I highly recommend using silicone bowls for melting candy wafers. Not only are the 1-cup silicone bowls the perfect size, but silicone helps to melt candy melts evenly and much faster than plastic, glass, or ceramic.

Toothpicks: These are the ultimate multipurpose tools for cake pop making. I cannot work without toothpicks, and I suggest you keep a few of them nearby when making your cake pops. I use them most for popping air bubbles on freshly coated cake pops, but they can also be used for fixing and filling cracks, guiding the candy coating off or onto an area of a cake pop, creating texture, and etching guidelines on cake pop designs that require precision piping or decorating.

Ziplock bags: These totally common kitchen items are rock stars in my cake pop world. Ziplock bags are what dreams and fine lines are made of! I use ziplock bags to pipe and add detail to my cake pops. I don't use any special tips or bags. Piping using candy coating is my preferred method for adding details on cake pops. This method works consistently, and there's no extra expense outside of materials that you're already using. Fill a corner of the bag with melted candy melts, twist to secure, snip off the corner with scissors, and you're ready to pipe!

Paramount crystals: Without these crystals, dipping cake pops would be very difficult. Paramount crystals are not actually crystals but are small, thin, and flat chips made from the same combination of oils found in candy coatings. The addition of paramount crystals in melted candy coating helps make each batch of candy coating fluid, thinner, creamier, and smooth without affecting the integrity of the candy coating once it sets and hardens. Add 1 teaspoon at a time during the candy coating melting process and stir well between each addition.

OTHER TOOLS AND EQUIPMENT

The following are other tools that you will need for making the cake pops in this book.

Stand mixer (optional): I did everything by hand for years before purchasing a stand mixer, but having one definitely makes the process easier.

Microwave: The easiest and my recommended way for melting candy coating.

Cookie sheet: Placing your cake balls or shapes on a wax paper–lined cookie sheet is ideal since the cake pops will make a couple of trips in and out of the refrigerator.

Mixing bowls: If you're making your cake pop dough completely by hand, you'll need at least one large bowl to do the mixing in.

Disposable gloves: I always use disposable gloves while making cake pops. I highly recommend you do so. A lot of direct food handling is done with the hands in the cake pop making process, and using disposable gloves helps prevent unwanted "ingredients" in your final product.

Paper lollipop sticks: White, 6-inch paper lollipop sticks are the standard type and size for cake pop making. Other lengths and other materials are available, like plastic or wood.

Styrofoam block or cake pop stand: This is an essential piece of cake pop making. You can easily stick your cake pops into a Styrofoam block to dry upright. A single Styrofoam block can be reused over and over again and will last a long while. See page 165 for information on cake pop stands.

Plastic wrap: Use this to cover cake pop dough while scooping the cake pop portions so the dough doesn't dry out. Also use for wrapping styrofoam blocks and stands for easy cleanup.

Cookie scoop: A standard cookie scoop, also called a cookie dropper, holds about 2 tablespoons, leveled.

Wilton Round Cut-Outs: This 3-piece set of stainless steel round cutters is handy in more ways than one. I like using them for cutting individual candy wafers as pieces for my cake pops.

Wax paper: Use wax paper to cover your work surface and to line cookie sheets before placing cake balls and shapes on them.

Paper straws: You can find paper straws in a variety of colors. I like using them for upside-down cake pops.

Paper towels: Keep them nearby for wiping your hands and tools.

Scissors: You will need scissors for preparing your piping bags and cutting candies.

Small sharp knife: Use this for cutting candy pieces and dividing cake pop balls.

Mini cocktail forks: These are used with the donut cake pops (pg. 115).

Chopsticks or popsicle sticks: I like using chopsticks or popsicle sticks for stirring candy

coating. They create less air bubbles, the straight edges allow you to scrape the sides of your dipping container easily, and the sticks themselves can be scraped off using the container rim, which leads to less waste.

Mini popsicle sticks: These are used with the popsicle cake pops (pg. 103).

Mini button mold: Use to make the wheels on the barbecue grill cake pops (pg. 109).

KRIS GALICIA BROWN

Making Cake Pop Dough

Dough: Crumbled cake + binder

Binder: Frosting, buttercream, or cream cheese

Cake pop dough consists of crumbled cake combined with a binder like frosting, buttercream, or even straight up cream cheese. Having perfect cake pop dough is the key and the foundation to making beautiful cake pops—it is the canvas where everything rests, including the stick. If the dough is the correct consistency, rolling balls and forming different shapes can be easy.

My ultimate rule #1: Do not follow cake pop recipes! As silly as that sounds, the reality is cake pop making is not a one-size-fits-all process. Not every cake yields 36 or 48 cake pops. Instead, follow a cake recipe and follow a binder recipe, or use boxed cake mix and creamy style, ready-made frosting. Then use your own judgment for the amount of binder to mix into the crumbled cake.

Every cake is unique. Cake consistencies vary depending on many different variables, like the type of cake, weather, altitude, time, and the actual temperature range of your oven. This is why it's so important to use your judgment when combining a binder into your crumbled cake rather than following exact, one-size-fits-all amounts.

All of the instructions in this book are for decorating 1 dozen cake pops in that particular design, so it will be much easier to follow, and they can be doubled or multiplied easily. (Please note that you can dip at least 2 dozen cake pops using 1 bag [16 ounces] of candy coating, even though only 1 dozen is listed in the instructions.)

CAKE HANDLING

Bake a cake from scratch or use a box mix and let it cool completely. And I mean completely! Each cake will yield different amounts of cake pops depending on the recipe and the kind of cake. This is because every cake flavor and every cake recipe will yield a different consistency. Chocolate and fruit-based cakes are naturally more moist and fluffy and therefore would need less of a binder, whereas denser cakes like red velvet or snickerdoodle cake would need more binder.

CRUMBLING AND CAKE RESERVE

Once the cake is completely cooled, crumble the cake with your hands or with a stand mixer at a low setting using the paddle attachment. Once the cake is crumbled, scoop out 1 cup and set it aside. This is what I call the "cake reserve." In case too much binder is added and you find your dough to be too sticky or tacky, this extra cup of crumbled cake might save you from baking another cake to remedy the "too wet and sticky" issue.

ADDING THE BINDER

The typical binder added to the crumbled cake is frosting or buttercream. I highly recommend using my cream cheese buttercream or honey buttercream. Cream cheese or store-bought rich and creamy–style frosting works as well. Cream cheese is a healthier option and works especially well with red velvet and chocolate cakes.

Start off by adding 3 tablespoons to ¼ cup of a binder to the crumbled cake. The amount of a binder depends on the type of cake, like I mentioned earlier. If you're working with a fruit-based cake or a really fluffy chocolate cake, start with about 3 tablespoons and gradually add more (if needed) to achieve the correct consistency. Combine by hand or with a stand mixer at a low setting using the paddle attachment. It will take a few minutes to fully combine. Continue to add 1 tablespoon of a binder at a time if needed. This takes time! A few minutes to get the dough perfect will save you so much time in the long run and will making rolling and shaping a breeze.

CORRECT TEXTURE

The correct texture and consistency is similar to that of play dough. The dough should not be tacky or sticky. If you place a ball of dough between your fingers and press, it should not crumble or have crumbs fall from it. Portions should also be easily rolled into a ball with minimal appearance of cracks or veinlike lines. If you find that the dough is too sticky, use that cake reserve! Add it in and combine it well with your hands or stand mixer, which should help remedy your sticky situation. If your dough is a bit dry or crumbly, add more binder, 1 tablespoon at a time.

If you're using a stand mixer, the dough should come together after a couple of minutes. If a couple of minutes have passed and your dough is still not at the proper consistency, add more binder, 1 tablespoon at a time, mixing between additions.

KRIS GALICIA BROWN

Rolling and Shaping the Dough

If you've taken all the previous steps, your cake pop dough should feel just like play dough. Once this consistency is achieved, gather the dough and form it into a giant ball and place on a piece of wax paper. Cover the top of the ball completely with plastic wrap. Plastic wrap will help keep the consistency of the dough and will also help it from drying out as you scoop and form shapes. You are now ready to roll and shape the dough! Use a cookie scoop to measure cake pop dough portions so all the cake pops are as uniform and even as possible. I use a standard metal cookie scoop, also called a cookie dropper, that yields 2 tablespoons of dough when leveled.

Lift the plastic wrap off of one side, scoop dough using your cookie scoop, level the dough using the palm of your hand, and release the dough from the scoop. Secure the plastic wrap around the remaining dough. Depending on the design of your cake pop, scoop only 1–3 portions, covering the dough after each scooping. If you find that your dough isn't nice and moldable halfway through the shaping process, add more binder to it, combine well, and rewrap in plastic wrap. Arrange rolled balls or sculpted shapes on a cookie sheet lined with wax paper.

Refrigerate the balls or shapes for at least 10 minutes before the next step: attaching sticks. Do not cover cookie sheet with plastic wrap or foil because condensation will collect along the top and drip onto your nicely rolled balls or shapes. Cover cookie sheet lightly with paper towels if desired.

Once the dough is shaped and refrigerated, altering the shape is not recommended; it will be difficult, so don't even try it. See the refrigeration and handling section on page 20 for tips on storing uncoated cake balls or shapes.

KRIS GALICIA BROWN

Assembling Cake Pops

ATTACHING THE STICKS

Always dip about ⅓ inch of the lollipop stick in melted candy coating just before inserting into the cake ball or shape. The coating will secure the cake ball or shape onto the stick, keeping it in place and preventing it from sliding. Insert the stick no more than halfway into the cake ball or shape. If you're making custom-shaped cake pops, find the center of gravity and insert the stick in that area. After inserting the sticks, place the cake pops in the fridge for a few minutes. Use this time to melt more candy wafers, to get the candy coating consistency as you like it, and to prep other materials.

CANDY COATING 101

Use deep containers instead of wide to melt your candy wafers. I highly recommend using small (1-cup) silicone bowls. Small plastic microwave-safe bowls or cups also work well. Avoid using glass or ceramic because these materials retain heat and then cool right away, affecting the candy melts' consistency.

I prefer the Merckens or Clasen brand of candy wafers. Please note that each color of each brand of candy coating melts into a different consistency. You may notice this especially with the darker colors, which can be more difficult to work with. Adding paramount crystals will help thin out the candy coating to your liking, even with the more difficult darker colors.

Start by microwaving the candy wafers in a silicone prep bowl or a microwave-safe container for 1 minute at 50 percent power. Stir. Then microwave at 30 second intervals at 50 percent power, stirring after each interval until you get a smooth consistency. Even if it looks like nothing has happened or changed much after each heating interval, please stir. The candy melts need to be moved around in your container to avoid scorching.

Use paramount crystals to thin out your candy melts until you reach a smooth and creamy consistency. Add about 1 teaspoon at a time and stir well. Microwave for 15 seconds at 50 percent power if needed, to help melt the added paramount crystals. If paramount crystals are unavailable in your area, you can order them online, or I suggest using vegetable shortening, but please note that you will not get the same results. Using large amounts of shortening will lengthen the amount of time it takes for your coating to set and might prevent the coating from hardening completely.

After microwaving, always let the melted candy coating rest at room temperature for at least 5 minutes before dipping.

CANDY COATING COLORS

Here's a visual reference list of all the candy wafer colors and candy wafer mixes used on the cake pops in this book.

CANDY WAFER COLORS

NO.	COLOR	NO.	COLOR	NO.	COLOR
1	super white	6	white	11	yellow
2	light pink	7	red	12	orange
3	hot pink	8	green	13	navy
4	butterscotch	9	purple	14	blue
5	chocolate	10	dark chocolate	15	black

KRIS GALICIA BROWN

CANDY WAFER MIXES

NO.	COLOR	NO.	COLOR	NO.	COLOR
1	**fried tan** 1 part chocolate + 1 part yellow + 2 parts white	4	**Granny Smith** 1 part green + 3 parts yellow	7	**dark night*** equal parts dark chocolate & navy
2	**roasted hazelnut** 1 part chocolate + 2 parts orange	5	**soft teal** 1 part green + 3 parts white + 4 parts blue	8	**blush pink**** 1 part hot pink + 4 parts white
3	**fire burst** 2 parts red + 3 parts orange	6	**soft charcoal** 1 part dark chocolate + 1 part navy + 2 parts white		*Substitute for black when dipping; the consistency is more ideal for dipping than black, which melts too thick. Dark night will look like a dark slate color when melted. The color will darken as it dries and with refrigeration. **Substitute if light pink is not available.

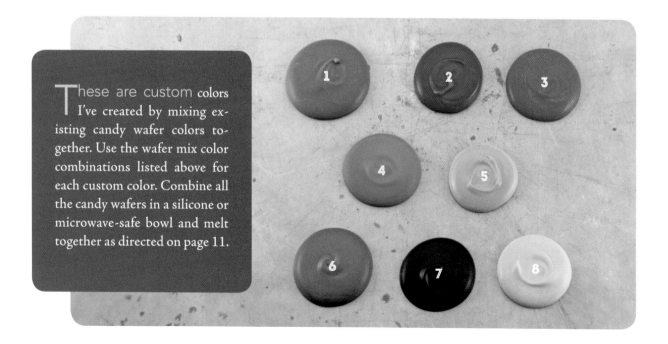

These are custom colors I've created by mixing existing candy wafer colors together. Use the wafer mix color combinations listed above for each custom color. Combine all the candy wafers in a silicone or microwave-safe bowl and melt together as directed on page 11.

DIPPING

The key element here is temperature. If the uncoated cake pops have been chilling in the refrigerator for an hour or more, let them rest at room temperature at least 5–10 minutes before dipping. This takes the chill off and helps minimize cracking. You may have to wait longer during colder weather. Working in small batches is always better as well. Remove 6–12 cake pops at a time from the refrigerator, depending on how quickly you can complete them.

The same rule goes for the candy coating. Let rest for 5–10 minutes before dipping. This further minimizes the chances of cracking.

Dunk the uncoated cake pop into the candy coating vertically until fully submerged. Pull out vertically and gently shake any excess coating off in an up-and-down motion while still upside down. Turn cake pop right side up and tap off any remaining excess coating using the side of the bowl or cup if necessary.

As you allow the excess coating to come off the cake pop, pop any air bubbles with the tip of a toothpick and lightly shake to allow the candy melt to evenly cover the area. Place cake pop on a Styrofoam block and let dry. You can also use a toothpick to gently help guide candy coating off a cake pop. Remember, you can always return to a cake pop to add more detail later!

DECORATING

Avoid hard candies and gum, like jawbreakers or cute round gumballs. They are choking hazards and all around hazardous. I also avoid using nuts because they are an allergen. I highly recommend against using them if you're making cake pops for a large crowd. You never know how sensitive your guests are to nuts. Always better to be safe than sorry.

If you're thinking about using candies on the surface, or exterior, of a cake pop, always test the new candies you want to use in the refrigerator first to see how they react to condensation. Put a few of the candies in a small container and place in the fridge for 20–30 minutes. Remove them from the fridge, let stand at room temperature for 15 minutes, and then take a look at them. Do the candies become too sticky? Did the colors run? Are they soggy or soft? You can then consider (or reconsider) using them for decorating your cake pops.

DRYING AND SETTING

Allow your cake pops to set, dry, and harden on a Styrofoam block or on a stand made for holding and positioning cake pops upright. Disposable cardboard cake pop stands are available at candy-making supply stores and craft stores as well.

It takes 1–2 minutes for the candy coating surface to set and another 2–3 minutes to dry and harden. Be careful not to accidentally touch your drying cake pops, especially when adding more freshly dipped cake pops to the Styrofoam block!

Here's a tip: Cover your Styrofoam block or stand in plastic wrap before each use. This helps to keep it clean and free from moisture and stains. Replace the plastic wrap after each use.

Decorating Sweets with Sweets

This is the colorful fun stuff that cake pop dreams are made of! So many different sprinkles, candies, and other goodies can be used to create endless designs. Three things I do not use in my cake pops: edible-ink pens, dye in my candy melts, and fondant. I like to keep it simple—no extra supplies to buy on top of what's already being used.

On the following pages are visual lists of decor, sprinkles, and candies and food items needed to make the cake pops in this book.

	OPTIONAL DECOR		
Nº.	ITEM	Nº.	ITEM
1	gold luster dust	3	navy disco dust
2	peacock-blue luster dust	4	gold disco dust

Sprinkles

Sprinkles come in so many different types. My favorites are sugar pearls and hearts. I like using black sugar pearls for eyes, and hearts work well as tiny noses and ears when placed upside down.

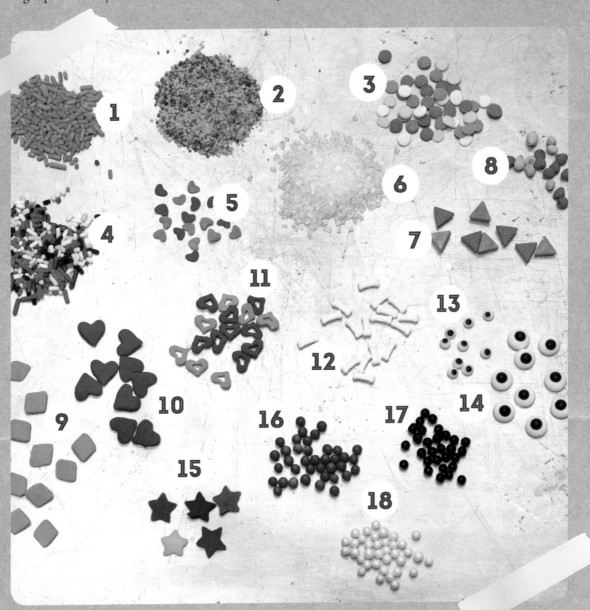

KRIS GALICIA BROWN

SPRINKLES

NO.	TYPE & USE	NO.	TYPE & USE	NO.	TYPE & USE
1	green jimmies	7	triangle sprinkles	13	2mm eye sprinkles
	Easter Baskets		Foxes		Ravens
2	toffee bits sprinkles	8	rainbow chip sprinkles	14	4mm eye sprinkles
	Starfish Beach		Chickens, Love Birds (orange & yellow sprinkles)		Love Birds, Owls
3	mini confetti sprinkles	9	jumbo diamond sprinkles	15	jumbo star sprinkles
	Cows, Holiday Trees		Strawberries (green sprinkles)		Holiday Trees
4	rainbow jimmies	10	jumbo heart sprinkles	16	blue sugar pearls
	Cows, Ice Cream Cones, Donuts		Love Birds		Ducks
5	mini heart sprinkles	11	hollow heart sprinkles	17	black sugar pearls
	Kittens, Rabbits, Chickens		Pigs		Malitpoos, Rabbits, Chickens, Ducks
6	white sugar crystals	12	miniature bones (seasonal—Halloween)	18	white sugar pearls
	Hearts		Roasted Turkeys		Sushi, Hot Air Balloons

CANDIES AND FOOD ITEMS

NO.	TYPE & USE	NO.	TYPE & USE	NO.	TYPE & USE
1	mini peanut butter cups Hot Air Balloons	8	cherry sours Ravens	15	chocolate eggs (Cadbury, seasonal) Easter Basket, Bird Nests
2	mallow bits Sheep	9	gummy worms Elephants	16	jelly beans (assorted) Easter Baskets, Bird Nests
3	M&M's Bears	10	candy corn Molars, Ravens	17	candy necklace pieces (orange) Lions
4	Starburst (pink and orange) Teacups, Ducks	11	jelly beans (black) Sheep	18	licorice nibs Pigs, Cows, Sheep
5	somen noodles Peacocks	12	Mike and Ike Malitpoos, Owls, Mittens	19	Twizzlers Pull-n-Peel Hot Chocolate Mugs, Teacups, Easter Baskets, Bananas
6	mini pretzel sticks Peacocks, Hearts, Broomsticks, Strawberries	13	Sixlets (white) Rabbits	20	black licorice string Giraffe
7	white or semisweet chocolate chips Kittens, Owls	14	gummy bears Sushi, Pineapples		

KRIS GALICIA BROWN

Candies and Food Items

Candy-hunting is my favorite part of the cake pop making process. I enjoy the simple pleasure of figuring out what candy pieces I can add to the design I'm imagining in my mind. My favorites are Mike and Ike, candy corn, and licorice. They're dynamic.

Refrigeration and Handling

COMPLETED CAKE POPS

Store completed cake pops in airtight containers with a paper towel between each layer. Always refrigerate cake pops—never freeze them. If the cake pops are individually wrapped in cellophane, they do not have to be placed in airtight containers. Place them in a baking tray or bakery box and refrigerate until the morning of use.

To thaw completed cake pops properly, remove the cake pops from the refrigerator and let sit at room temperature for at least 1–2 hours before handing. Do *not* touch or handle them at all during this time. This will allow the condensation from the cake pops to collect and dry completely without leaving a sticky residue.

UNCOATED CAKE BALLS OR SHAPES

If being dipped within 2–3 days, uncoated cake balls and shapes should be stored in a single layer in an airtight container in the refrigerator. If long-term storage is desired, freeze cake balls or shapes in a single layer for a few hours. Once completely frozen, place cake balls in labeled and dated resealable freezer bags. Keep frozen for up to 2 months.

To thaw from frozen, arrange frozen cake balls or shapes in a single layer on a paper towel–lined cookie sheet or baking pan. Cover them loosely with another paper towel and place in the refrigerator for a few hours or at room temperature for 30–45 minutes. Attach sticks and dip as usual.

KRIS GALICIA BROWN

Troubleshooting

WHAT SHOULD I DO IF MY CAKE POP DOUGH CRUMBLES WHEN I TRY TO ROLL THE BALLS OR MAKE SHAPES?

Your dough isn't at the right consistency yet. You want it to feel similar to play dough. Add more binder to your dough, 1 tablespoon at a time, and mix thoroughly. Remember to cover your dough in plastic wrap as you scoop and roll so the dough doesn't dry out (pg. 9).

WHAT SHOULD I DO IF MY CAKE POP DOUGH IS TOO STICKY AND WET?

If the dough is too sticky, you've added too much binder and you now need to add more cake. Use your cake reserve: get into the habit of scooping out about 1 cup of crumbled cake just before you add any kind of binder to it; otherwise, if your dough ends up too sticky, you'll need to bake another cake, crumble down a small portion of it, and add it in.

HOW LONG DO CAKE POPS USUALLY TAKE TO DRY?

It takes 1–2 minutes for the candy coating surface to set and another 2–3 minutes to dry and harden completely.

WHY IS MY PIPING CAUSING CRACKS ON THE COATING?

The candy coating in the piping bag is too warm. Let it rest for a minute and then continue to pipe.

WHY DOES MY COATING LOOK LIKE ITS SAGGING?

The cake pop is too cold, so the coating is setting unevenly. Let your uncoated cake pops sit at room temperature for a couple of minutes before continuing to dip.

HOW DO I MAKE MY CAKE POPS LOOK SMOOTH?

The secret is in the dough. If your dough is smooth, your cake pops will be as well. Also, make sure to thin out your candy coating using paramount crystals until the coating is thin and smooth. The perfect candy coating consistency to work with is dark chocolate or white.

WHY ARE MY CAKE POPS CRACKING AFTER I COAT THEM?

Cracks are caused by one of two things: temperature, which is the most common cause, or cracks on the surface of the *uncoated* cake pop. It's important to find a good balance of temperatures between the uncoated cake pop and the candy coating, and to let your cake pops rest after refrigeration or after microwaving.

Temperature: As mentioned previously, after removing uncoated cake pops from the refrigerator, let them sit at room temperature for at least 5–10 minutes or more if they were in the refrigerator longer than a few hours. After melting the candy wafers in the microwave and getting it to your desired dipping consistency, let it rest at room temperature for about 5 minutes before dipping.

Surface cracks: Another cause for cracks in the coating is cracks on the uncoated cake ball or shape. If you notice a deep crack on your uncoated cake pop, use a toothpick to fill the cavity with melted candy coating and smooth it over with your finger. Let it dry completely and then dip as usual.

I HAVE OIL OOZING OUT OF A CRACK OR SMALL HOLE IN MY CAKE POP. WHAT IS THAT, AND HOW CAN I FIX IT?

The oozing is oil from the cake pop dough coming to room temperature within the candy coating. The oil most likely pushed through an air bubble in the coating or through a crack. Place the cake pop on a paper towel, crack or hole side down, and the oozing will stop after a little while. Let it ooze out, and come back to it later. When the oozing stops, use a toothpick to fill the crack or hole with candy coating and, after it has dried completely, use a clean, dry paper towel as "sandpaper" and carefully smooth the coating on the surface where you filled the crack. Don't try to fix the hole or crack while it's still oozing—the ooze will push through the patch of coating every time.

WHAT IS THE BEST WAY TO STORE CAKE POPS?

See page 20.

HOW DO I FIX THE CRACKS ON THE COATING?

If your coating cracks, there are a couple of ways you may be able to fix it. Double-dipping is one way. You can dip your cake pop again, but note that this cake pop will look bigger than the others. Another way of fixing the crack is to take a toothpick and fill the crack with candy coating. Then when it has dried completely, use a clean, dry paper towel as "sandpaper" and carefully smooth the coating on the surface where you filled the crack.

Cake Pop BASICS

In this section, you'll find the how-tos of cake pop making. We'll cover piping, preparing a piping bag with candy coating, and making basic traditional (upright) cake pops and upside-down cake pops.

Piping

Don't let piping intimidate you. Piping takes a bit of practice, but it's a skill that's easily polished. Practice control by laying out a piece of wax paper and piping small swirls, shapes, letters, and other patterns on it. Let it dry, break it up, melt it again, and start over. By doing this, you're learning by muscle memory how to hold, angle, and squeeze as you form designs. You can also familiarize yourself with the different sizes of lines you can pipe by continually snipping off the corner of the bag tiny bits at a time.

PREPARING A PIPING BAG IS EASY.

You'll need:

a small or short drinking glass • a sandwich-sized ziplock bag • melted candy wafers • scissors

Use a small drinking glass to position the bag open by inserting one corner of the bag into the glass and folding the bag, cuffing the opening outward and over the glass rim. Pour melted candy coating into the bag, remove bag from the glass, squeeze out air, and twist. Using scissors, snip off a tiny portion of the corner when you're ready to pipe.

If you find your candy coating hardening, microwave the ziplock bag for 10 seconds at 50 percent power. Then pinch the opening with the fingers of one hand and use the fingers of your other hand to knead the candy coating in the bag so that the consistency is even throughout. Repeat if necessary.

Tip: Temperature is key! Always let the candy coating bag rest for a couple of minutes before piping. If the candy coating is too warm, it will cause cracks on your beautifully coated cake pop.

KRIS GALICIA BROWN

WET-ON-WET PIPING TECHNIQUE

This technique allows you to create cake pops with piped lines or piped designs that are flush with the surface. The secret to this technique is that the candy coatings have to be very close to the same consistency.

You'll need:

- 12 uncoated round cake balls, chilled
- 16 oz. (1 lb.) candy wafers in any color

- silicone prep bowl or a deep microwave-safe plastic bowl or cup
- paramount crystals (optional)

- 12 paper lollipop sticks
- toothpicks
- prepared piping bag
- Styrofoam block

DECORATING

Remove round cake balls from the refrigerator and let rest at room temperature for about 10 minutes.

Melt the candy wafers in a silicone bowl or in a microwave-safe plastic bowl or cup. Refer to page 11 for melting instructions and tips. Thin coating if necessary by adding paramount crystals 1 teaspoon at a time; stir to mix well.

One at a time, dip the tip of each paper lollipop stick into the melted candy coating, about ⅓ inch, and insert the stick into the bottom (small flat portion that rested on the baking sheet) of a round cake ball, pushing it about ¾ inch, or about halfway, through the ball.

Once all the sticks have been inserted, stir the melted candy coating to make sure the consistency is even before starting to dip the cake pops. Then, one at a time, dip each ball into the candy coating vertically until fully submerged. Pull out vertically and gently shake any excess coating off in an up-and-down motion while still upside down. Turn cake pops right side up and tap off any remaining excess coating using the side of the bowl or cup.

As you allow the excess melts to come off of the cake pop, pop any air bubbles with the tip of a toothpick and lightly shake to allow the candy melts to evenly cover the area. Do not wait for the cake pop to dry.

One at a time, hold each cake pop by the stick in one hand and hold the piping bag in the other hand. Pipe drizzles around the cake pop by using your fingers to twist the stick as you pipe in a back and forward motion all over the cake pop. Or pipe random or symmetric swirls.

Place cake pops on the Styrofoam block and let dry completely.

KRIS GALICIA BROWN

BASIC CAKE POPS

You'll need:

- 12 uncoated round cake balls, chilled
- 1 (16-oz.) bag candy wafers in any color
- silicone bowl, or a deep microwave-safe plastic bowl or cup
- 12 paper lollipop sticks
- paramount crystals
- toothpicks
- sprinkles (optional)
- prepared piping bag (optional)
- Styrofoam block

DECORATING

Remove round cake balls from the refrigerator and let rest at room temperature for about 10 minutes.

Melt the candy wafers in a silicone bowl or microwave-safe plastic bowl or cup. Refer to page 11 for melting instructions and tips. Thin coating if necessary by adding paramount crystals 1 teaspoon at a time. Stir to mix well.

One at a time, dip the tip of each paper lollipop stick into the melted candy coating, about ⅓ inch, and insert the stick into the bottom (small flat portion that rested on the baking sheet) of a round cake ball, pushing it about ¾ inch, or about halfway, through the ball.

Once all the sticks have been inserted, stir the melted candy coating to make sure the consistency is even before starting to dip the cake pops. Then, one at a time, dip each ball into the candy coating vertically until fully submerged. Pull out vertically and gently shake any excess coating off in an up-and-down motion, while still upside down. Turn right side up and tap off any remaining excess coating using the side of the bowl or cup.

As you allow the excess melts to come off the cake pop, pop any air bubbles with the tip of a toothpick and lightly shake to allow the candy melts to evenly cover the area.

Add decoration as desired. If adding sprinkles, sprinkle coated cake pop before it sets and hardens. Work over a bowl or plate to catch the excess sprinkles. If you find that the sprinkles are causing "sagging" throughout your coating, wait a few seconds longer before sprinkling. Also, see pages 24 and 25 for piping instructions and options.

Place cake pops on the Styrofoam block.

UPSIDE-DOWN CAKE POPS

You'll need:

- 12 uncoated round cake balls, chilled
- 1 (16-oz.) bag candy wafers in any color
- paramount crystals
- silicone bowl, or a deep microwave-safe plastic bowl or cup
- wax paper
- 12 paper lollipop sticks or paper straws
- toothpicks
- sprinkles (optional)
- prepared piping bag (optional)

DECORATING:

Remove round cake balls from the refrigerator and let rest at room temperature for about 10 minutes.

Melt the candy wafers in a silicone bowl or in a microwave-safe plastic bowl or cup. Refer to page 11 for melting instructions and tips. Thin coating if necessary by adding paramount crystals 1 teaspoon at a time. Stir to mix well.

Lay a piece of wax paper aside on your flat work surface. One at a time, dip the tip of each paper lollipop stick (see next paragraph for paper straws) into the melted candy coating, about ⅓ inch, and insert the stick into the top of a round cake ball, pushing it about ¾ inch, or about halfway, through the ball.

If you're using paper straws, carefully dip or dab candy coating on the top of each cake ball and then dip the tip of each paper straw into the melted candy coating, about ⅓ inch, and insert the straw into the top of the cake ball, pushing it about ¾ inch, or about halfway, through the ball. This ensures there aren't any uncoated areas, including the enclosed center area of the straw, where oil can seep through.

Once all the sticks or straws have been inserted, stir the melted candy coating to make sure the consistency is even before starting to dip the cake pops. Then, one at a time, dip each ball into the candy coating vertically until fully submerged. Pull out vertically and gently shake any excess coating off in an up-and-down motion while still upside down. Gently place the cake ball portion on the wax paper and help to balance it vertically by holding the tip of the stick if necessary.

Add decoration as desired. If using sprinkles, sprinkle coated cake pop before it sets and hardens. If you find that the sprinkles are causing "sagging" throughout your coating, wait a few seconds longer before sprinkling. Also, see pages 24 and 25 for piping instructions and options.

KRIS GALICIA BROWN

CAKE POP BASICS

Custom
CAKE POPS

maltipoo

KRIS GALICIA BROWN

MALTIPOOS

You'll need:

- 12 uncoated shaped cake balls and snouts, chilled
- small sharp knife
- wax paper
- cookie sheet
- 1½ bags (24 oz.) super white candy wafers
- silicone bowl, or a deep microwave-safe plastic bowl or cup
- paramount crystals
- 12 Mike and Ike candies
- 12 paper lollipop sticks
- toothpicks
- 24 black sugar pearls
- prepared piping bag containing black candy coating
- Styrofoam block

PREPARATION:

Using a cookie scoop, scoop and shape cake pop dough into balls. On each ball, slice off ¼ inch of the dough. Roll the tiny sliced portion into a dome shape; this will form the maltipoo's snout. Place on a wax paper–lined cookie sheet. Chill in the refrigerator for 10–15 minutes.

While the dough chills, melt the super white candy wafers in a silicone bowl or a microwave-safe plastic bowl or cup. Thin the consistency with paramount crystals if necessary and let rest at room temperature for at least 5 minutes before dipping.

Using the knife once more, cut the Mike and Ike candies lengthwise at a diagonal. These will be the ears.

DECORATING:

Remove the round cake balls and snouts from the refrigerator. Let rest at room temperature for a few minutes. Dip about ⅓ inch of one end of the lollipop stick into the candy coating and then insert a stick into the middle of each ball, with the flat side facing backward. The flat side will be the back of the head. Push until the stick is about halfway through the ball.

Attach the snouts on the faces by using a toothpick to dab a small amount of candy coating onto the center of each ball and attaching the snout in that area.

Once you've attached all the sticks and snouts, refrigerate the pops for 2–3 minutes to harden the candy coating.

When you're ready to dip, hold the cake pop stick vertically, with the cake pop upside down. Dip into super white candy coating. Submerge completely and pull out. Lightly wiggle to allow the excess coating to slide off the top. Use a toothpick to pierce any air bubbles stuck in the coating or to guide excess candy coating off the cake pop. Turn right side up and continue to tap off the excess using the rim of your bowl.

While cake pop is still wet, attach two black pearls (eyes) evenly just above the snout, in the crease where the snout meets the head. Attach the thinner side of the diagonally cut Mike and Ike candies on either side of the head to make ears.

Using the prepared piping bag filled with black candy coating, pipe an upside down triangle at the top tip of the snout.

Finally, using a toothpick, carefully dab super white coating on the face, creating texture with the toothpick. Take your time and be careful around the eyes and nose. Cover the ears, making sure the under part is well covered, and the rest of the head in this manner. The more you dab, the more realistic the "fur" will be.

KITTENS

You'll need:

- 12 uncoated oval-shaped cake balls, chilled
- wax paper
- cookie sheet
- 1 (16-oz.) bag light pink candy wafers
- silicone bowl, or a deep microwave-safe plastic bowl or cup
- paramount crystals
- 12 paper lollipop sticks
- 24 white or semisweet chocolate chips (use white for lighter-colored cake pop dough or semisweet for darker-colored cake pop dough)
- toothpicks
- Styrofoam block
- prepared piping bag containing chocolate candy coating
- 12 mini pink heart sprinkles
- prepared piping bag containing super white candy coating

PREPARATION:

Using a cookie scoop, scoop and shape cake pop dough into ovals. Place on a wax paper–lined cookie sheet. Chill in the refrigerator for 10–15 minutes.

While the dough chills, melt the light pink candy wafers in a silicone bowl or a microwave-safe plastic bowl or cup. Thin the consistency with paramount crystals if necessary and let rest at room temperature for at least 5 minutes before dipping.

DECORATING:

Remove the oval cake balls from the refrigerator. Let rest at room temperature for a few minutes. Dip about ⅓ inch of one end of the lollipop stick into the candy coating and then insert into the middle of the oval shape along the long side. Push until the stick is about halfway through the oval.

Attach two chocolate chips on the top of each oval by dabbing a small amount of candy coating with a toothpick onto the top of the oval and placing chocolate chips. These will be the kitten's ears.

Once you've attached all the sticks and chocolate chips, refrigerate the cake pops for 2–3 minutes to help harden the candy coating. If you notice that the candy coating is already hardened and set, you're ready to dip!

Hold the cake pop stick vertically, with the cake pop upside down. Dip into light pink candy coating. Submerge completely and pull out. Lightly wiggle to allow the excess coating to slide off the top. Use a toothpick to pierce any air bubbles stuck in the coating or to guide excess candy coating off the cake pop. Turn cake pops right side up, continue to tap off the excess coating using the rim of your bowl, and place pop on a Styrofoam block to dry.

Using the prepared piping bag filled with chocolate candy coating, pipe two dots for eyes.

Beginners: Using a toothpick, dab a dot of light pink candy coating on the center of the oval and attach a mini pink heart for its nose.

Using the prepared piping bag filled with super white candy coating, pipe three lines for whiskers on each side of the face.

Advanced: Using the prepared piping bag filled with super white candy coating, pipe an oval in the center of the face. Then pipe three lines radiating from the oval, for whiskers, on each side of the face. Attach a mini pink heart sprinkle in the upper center portion of the white piped oval.

kitten

rabbit

KRIS GALICIA BROWN

RABBITS

You'll need:

- 12 uncoated round cake balls, chilled
- wax paper
- cookie sheet
- 1 (16-oz.) bag super white candy wafers
- silicone bowl, or a deep microwave-safe plastic bowl or cup
- paramount crystals
- small sharp knife
- 12 super white candy wafers discs
- 1½-inch fondant cutter (medium Wilton Cut-Out from the 3-piece set, pg. 4)
- 12 paper lollipop sticks
- 12 Sixlet candies, white
- toothpicks
- 24 black sugar pearls
- Styrofoam block
- 12 mini pink hearts
- prepared piping bag containing black candy coating

PREPARATION:

Using a cookie scoop, scoop and shape cake pop dough into balls. Place on a wax paper–lined cookie sheet. Chill in the refrigerator for 10–15 minutes.

While the dough chills, melt the super white candy wafers in the microwave in a silicone bowl. Thin the consistency with paramount crystals if necessary and let rest at room temperature for at least 5 minutes before dipping.

Using a small sharp knife, cut each of the 12 super white candy wafers in half. Then, using the rounded edge of the 1½-inch round fondant cutter, trim the straight edges of each wafer half to create rabbit ears.

DECORATING:

Remove the cake balls from the refrigerator. Let rest at room temperature for a few minutes. Dip about ⅓ inch of one end of the lollipop stick into the candy coating and then insert into the bottom of the cake pop and push until the stick is about halfway through the ball.

Once you've attached all the sticks, refrigerate the cake pops for 2–3 minutes to harden the candy coating. Remove from the fridge and, on each cake pop, make an indentation using a Sixlet candy in the middle on one side of the ball. This will serve as a guide for placing the tail and will also help hold it in place.

When you're ready to dip, hold the cake pop stick vertically, with the cake pop upside down. Dip into super white candy coating. Submerge completely and pull out. Lightly wiggle to allow the excess coating to slide off the top. Use a toothpick to pierce any air bubbles stuck in the coating or to guide excess candy coating off the cake pop. Turn right side up and affix a Sixlet candy in the indentation you made earlier. On the opposite end, attach two black pearls (eyes) on the face and push the two ears into the top of the cake ball.

Let cake pops dry completely on the Styrofoam block. Use a toothpick to place a dot of candy coating on the middle of the face and attach a pink heart nose.

Using the prepared piping bag filled with black candy coating, pipe three lines for whiskers on each side of the face.

KRIS GALICIA BROWN

CHICKENS

You'll need:

- 12 uncoated cake balls shaped into thick crescents, chilled
- wax paper
- cookie sheet
- 1 (16-oz.) bag super white candy wafers

- silicone bowl, or a deep microwave-safe plastic bowl or cup
- paramount crystals
- 12 paper lollipop sticks
- toothpicks

- 48 red mini heart sprinkles
- 12 orange rainbow chip sprinkles
- 24 black sugar pearls
- Styrofoam block

PREPARATION:

Using a cookie scoop, scoop and shape cake pop dough into a fat crescent shape, making sure the middle area is thicker than the ends. The best way to do this is to roll into an oval first and then use your fingers to elongate and taper the ends into a crescent shape. Place on a wax paper–lined cookie sheet. Chill in the refrigerator for 10–15 minutes.

While the dough chills, melt the super white candy wafers in the microwave in a silicone bowl. Thin the consistency with paramount crystals if necessary and let rest at room temperature for at least 5 minutes before dipping.

DECORATING:

Remove the crescent shapes from the refrigerator. Let rest at room temperature for a few minutes. Holding the crescents with the ends upward, find the center of gravity in the center. Dip about ⅓ inch of one end of the lollipop stick into the candy coating and then insert into the bottom center and straight up into the middle of the cake pop.

Once you've attached all the sticks, refrigerate the cake pops for 2–3 minutes to help set the candy coating. Remove from the fridge.

When you're ready to dip, hold the cake pop stick vertically, with the cake pop upside down. Dip into candy coating. Submerge completely and pull out.

Lightly wiggle to allow the excess coating to slide off the top edge. Use a toothpick to pierce any air bubbles stuck in the coating or to guide excess candy coating off the cake pop. Turn right side up and continue to tap off excess if necessary.

While the coating is still wet, attach 3 mini hearts, pointed side down, in a line along the top of the chicken's head. Carefully affix the black pearl eyes, orange chip beaks, and another mini heart (upside down) to the face. If you don't like where you've placed one of the small pieces, use the tip of a toothpick to help guide it to where you want it.

Place cake pops in Styrofoam block and let dry completely.

chicken

sheep and pigs

SHEEP

You'll need:

- 12 uncoated cake balls shaped into ovals, chilled
- wax paper
- cookie sheet
- 1 (16-oz.) bag super white candy wafers
- ¼ bag (4 oz.) black candy wafers

- 2 silicone bowls, or deep microwave-safe plastic bowls or cups
- paramount crystals
- toothpicks
- 48 licorice nibs
- 12 paper lollipop sticks
- 12 large black jelly beans

- 1 (3-oz.) container Jet-Puffed Mallow Bits
- Styrofoam block
- prepared piping bag containing super white candy coating

PREPARATION:

Using a cookie scoop, scoop and shape cake pop dough into ovals. Place on a wax paper–lined cookie sheet. Chill in the refrigerator for 10–15 minutes.

While the dough chills, melt the super white candy wafers and black candy wafer mix separately in microwave in silicone bowls. Thin the consistency with paramount crystals if necessary and let rest at room temperature for at least 5 minutes before dipping.

Push one toothpick into an end of each licorice nib. Dip each nib into the black candy coating, but only dip until the edge—do not submerge completely. Place nibs on Styrofoam block and let dry completely. Once dry, remove the toothpicks.

DECORATING:

Remove the oval-shaped cake balls from the refrigerator. Let rest at room temperature for a few minutes. Dip about ⅓ inch of one end of the lollipop stick into the candy coating and then, with the oval lying horizontally, insert stick into the middle of the oval and push until the stick is about halfway through.

Once you've attached all the sticks, refrigerate the cake pops for 2–3 minutes to harden the candy coating. Remove from the fridge and, on each cake pop, use a jelly bean to make an indentation in the middle of the round end of the oval. This will serve as a guide for placing the head and will also help hold it in place.

When you're ready to dip, hold the cake pop stick vertically, with the cake pop upside down. Dip into super white candy coating. Submerge completely and pull out. Lightly wiggle to allow the excess coating to slide off the top. Use a toothpick to pierce any air bubbles stuck in the coating or to guide excess candy coating off the cake pop.

While the coating is still wet, place a black jelly bean in the indentation you made earlier. Carefully place four nibs (legs) on the under part of the oval, attaching the red uncoated ends onto the body.

Take advantage of the wet coating and apply as many Mallow Bits as you can, in a single layer, over the sheep's entire body. If the coating hardens, use a prepared piping bag filled with super white candy coating to spread candy coating in areas that still need to be covered in Mallow Bits.

Finally, pipe 2 eyes and a smile on the jelly bean head of each sheep.

PIGS

You'll need:

- 12 uncoated cake balls shaped into ovals, chilled
- wax paper
- cookie sheet
- 16 oz. "blush pink" candy wafer mix (pg. 13)

- silicone bowl, or a deep microwave-safe plastic bowl or cup
- paramount crystals
- small sharp knife
- 27 licorice nibs

- 12 paper lollipop sticks
- toothpicks
- 24 pink hollow hearts
- 24 black sugar pearls
- Styrofoam block

PREPARATION:

Using a cookie scoop, scoop and shape cake pop dough into ovals. Place on a wax paper–lined cookie sheet. Chill in the refrigerator for 10–15 minutes.

While the dough chills, melt the "blush pink" candy wafer mix in the microwave in a silicone bowl. Thin the consistency with paramount crystals if necessary and let rest at room temperature for at least 5 minutes before dipping. I use the blush pink wafer mix because the color matches the pinkness of the heart ears.

Using a small sharp knife, cut 24 licorice nibs in half, crosswise, for a total of 48 pieces (for the legs). Then cut the remaining 3 nibs into fourths, crosswise, for a total of 12 pieces (for the snouts).

DECORATING:

Remove the oval-shaped cake balls from the refrigerator. Let rest at room temperature for a few minutes. Dip about ⅓ inch of one end of the lollipop stick into the candy coating and then, with the oval lying horizontally, insert stick into the middle and push until it's about halfway through the shape.

Next, attach 4 licorice nib leg halves onto the bottoms of each oval, by dabbing candy coating and affixing the cut side of the nibs to the cake ball. Attach a licorice nib snout in the same manner on the rounded end of the oval.

Once you've attached all the sticks, legs, and snouts, refrigerate the cake pops for 2–3 minutes to harden the candy coating.

When you're ready to dip, hold the cake pop stick vertically, with the cake pop upside down. Dip into candy coating. Submerge completely and pull out. Lightly wiggle to allow the excess coating to slide off the top. Use a toothpick to pierce any air bubbles stuck in the coating or to guide excess candy coating off the cake pop. Turn right side up and place the heart sprinkles upside down on the top of the end where the snout is to create the pig's ears. Place 2 black sugar pearls just above the snout to give the pig some eyes. Do this for every cake pop.

COWS

You'll need:

- 12 uncoated cake balls shaped into ovals, chilled
- wax paper
- cookie sheet
- 1 (16-oz.) bag super white candy wafers
- silicone bowl, or a deep microwave-safe plastic bowl or cup
- paramount crystals

- small sharp knife
- 24 licorice nibs
- $5/8$-inch and $1½$-inch fondant cutters (small and medium Wilton Cut-Outs from the 3-piece set, pg. 4)
- 12 butterscotch or peanut butter candy wafers
- 12 paper lollipop sticks

- toothpicks
- 24 white mini confetti sprinkles
- 24 yellow jimmies
- Styrofoam block
- prepared piping bag containing chocolate candy coating
- prepared piping bag containing black candy coating

PREPARATION:

Using a cookie scoop, scoop and shape cake pop dough into ovals. Place on a wax paper–lined cookie sheet. Chill in the refrigerator for 10–15 minutes.

While the dough chills, melt the super white candy wafers in the microwave in a silicone bowl. Thin the consistency with paramount crystals if necessary and let rest at room temperature for at least 5 minutes before dipping.

Using a small sharp knife, cut 24 licorice nibs in half, crosswise, for a total of 48 pieces (for the legs).

Using the small fondant cutter, cut each butterscotch or peanut butter wafer into a smaller circle. Use the rounded edge of the 1½-inch round fondant cutter to trim an edge of each small wafer circle. These will be used for the cow snouts.

DECORATING:

Remove the oval-shaped cake balls from the refrigerator. Let rest at room temperature for a few minutes. Dip about ⅓ inch of one end of the lollipop stick into the candy coating and then, with the oval laying horizontally, insert stick into the middle and push until stick is about halfway through the shape.

Next, attach 4 licorice nib leg halves onto the bottoms of each oval by dabbing in candy coating and affixing the cut side to the cake ball.

Once you've attached all the sticks and legs, refrigerate cake pops for 2–3 minutes to help harden the candy coating.

When you're ready to dip, hold the cake pop stick vertically, with the cake pop upside down. Dip into candy coating. Submerge completely and pull out. Lightly wiggle to allow the excess coating to slide off the top. Use a toothpick to pierce any air bubbles stuck in the coating or to guide candy coating off the cake pop.

Turn right side up and, while the coating is still wet, place two confetti sprinkles on the top of the round end of the oval to create the cow's ears. Push two yellow jimmies in the inner area between the ears.

Next, attach the snout with the trimmed side up in the middle of the face. Let dry completely on a Styrofoam block.

Finally, using the piping bag with chocolate candy coating, pipe two small oval eyes just above the snout. Then, using the piping bag with black candy coating, pipe black spots randomly all over the cow's body.

KRIS GALICIA BROWN

pigs and cows

bear

KRIS GALICIA BROWN

BEARS

You'll need:

- 12 uncoated cake balls shaped into ovals, chilled
- wax paper
- cookie sheet
- 1 (16-oz.) bag hot pink candy wafers
- silicone bowl, or a deep microwave-safe plastic bowl or cup
- paramount crystals
- 12 paper lollipop sticks
- 24 M&M's
- toothpicks
- Styrofoam block
- prepared piping bag containing super white candy coating, about 10 wafers
- prepared piping bag containing black candy coating, about 10 wafers

PREPARATION:

Using a cookie scoop, scoop and shape cake pop dough into ovals. Place on a wax paper–lined cookie sheet. Chill in the refrigerator for 10–15 minutes.

While the dough chills, melt the hot pink candy wafers in the microwave in a silicone bowl. Thin the consistency with paramount crystals if necessary and let rest at room temperature for at least 5 minutes before dipping.

DECORATING:

Remove the oval cake balls from the refrigerator. Let rest at room temperature for a few minutes. Dip about ⅓ inch of one end of the lollipop stick into the candy coating and then insert into the middle of the oval shape along the long side. Push until the stick is about halfway through the oval.

Once you've attached all the sticks, refrigerate the cake pops for 2–3 minutes to help harden the candy coating.

Remove from the fridge. Gently push two M&M's ⅓ of the way in vertically on the top outer sides of the oval to create an indentation. Remove them, dip the edge of the M&M's into candy coating, and push back into the indentations. These will be the bear ears.

When you're ready to dip, hold the cake pop stick vertically, with the cake pop upside down. Dip into hot pink candy coating. Submerge completely and pull out. Lightly wiggle to allow the excess coating to slide off the top. Use a toothpick to pierce any air bubbles stuck in the coating or to guide excess candy coating off the cake pop. Turn right side up and continue to tap the excess using the rim of your bowl and place cake pops on a Styrofoam block to dry.

Using the piping bag with super white candy coating, pipe an oval in the center of the face.

Finally, using the piping bag with black candy coating, pipe a small oval nose in the center of the large white oval. Pipe two eyes above the nose.

PEACOCKS

You'll need:

- 12 uncoated cake balls, shaped like a coach's whistle, chilled; plus 3 more cake balls
- wax paper
- cookie sheet
- small sharp knife
- 1 (16-oz.) bag blue candy wafers
- silicone bowl, or a deep microwave-safe plastic bowl or cup
- paramount crystals
- 6 mini pretzel sticks
- somen noodles
- 12 paper lollipop sticks
- toothpicks
- Styrofoam block
- prepared piping bag containing blue candy coating
- prepared piping bag containing black candy coating
- disco dust, navy

Optional:

- large brush with nylon bristles
- luster dust, peacock blue
- disco dust, gold

PREPARATION

Using a cookie scoop, scoop and shape cake pop dough into 12 rounded wedges, similar to a coach's whistle. Place on a wax paper–lined cookie sheet. Chill in the refrigerator for 10–15 minutes.

Scoop an additional 3 portions and roll into balls. Using a small sharp knife, split each ball into eighths: Cut in half, and cut each half down the center vertically and horizontally. There should be a total of 24 pieces. Shape 12 into mini droplets, which will be the peacock heads, and chill in the refrigerator. The remaining 12 will be used for the necks. Keep these at room temperature.

While the dough chills, melt the blue candy wafers in microwave in silicone bowl. Thin the consistency with paramount crystals if necessary and let rest

DECORATING:

Remove the whistle-shaped wedges and small droplets from the refrigerator. Let rest at room temperature for a few minutes. Dip about ⅓ inch of one end of the lollipop stick into the candy coating and then, with the whistle-shaped wedge pointing downward, insert the stick vertically into the middle from the bottom and push up until the stick is about halfway through (see photo for stick placement).

Then dip the tip of each pretzel piece and push it into the top of the body, sticking out of the body vertically. This will be the skeleton of the neck. If you feel the neck is too long, carefully snap off a piece of the pretzel.

Take one of the room-temperature cake pieces, flatten it with your fingers, and wrap it around the exposed pretzel stick, smoothing it around the pretzel as best you can and leaving ⅛-inch portion of the pretzel stick still exposed at the top edge. This is where the head will be placed, so covering it with dough isn't necessary. You will not have to use the cake piece. Only use enough to cover and smooth out the pretzel rod.

Next, lay the droplet piece horizontally with the pointed end facing forward and then push onto the exposed part of the neck. Once you've attached all the sticks, necks, and heads, refrigerate for 2–3 minutes to help harden the candy coating.

When you're ready to dip, hold the cake pop stick vertically, with the cake pop upside down. Dip into

at room temperature for at least 5 minutes before dipping. Snap each pretzel rod into 2 pieces. Snap a few somen noodles into ½-inch pieces.

candy coating; submerge completely and pull out. Lightly wiggle, being very gentle, to allow the excess coating to slide off the top. Use a toothpick to pierce any air bubbles stuck in the coating or to guide excess candy coating off of the cake pop.

Turn right side up. While the coating is still wet, insert 4 pieces of somen noodles on top of the head to form the crest. Adjust the height of the crest by snapping off small pieces at a time. Place on a Styrofoam block to dry.

Using the piping bag with blue candy coating, pipe rounded diamond shapes along the back of the body.

Pipe wing-tip eyes using the piping bag with black candy coating.

Dot the tips of the crest using a prepared piping bag and dip the tips into navy disco dust.

Optional: (Luster dust and disco dust are non-toxic and are for decorational purposes.) Use a fine nylon bristle brush to brush the peacocks with peacock blue luster dust.

Using the prepared piping bag containing blue candy coating, dot the upper area of each rounded diamond shape along the back and sprinkle with navy disco dust. Let dry and brush off excess with the fine nylon brush.

Dot the bottom area of the rounded diamonds and sprinkle with gold disco dust.

peacock

CUSTOM CAKE POPS

giraffes

KRIS GALICIA BROWN

GIRAFFES

You'll need:

- 12 uncoated cake balls, shaped like rounded droplets, chilled
- wax paper
- cookie sheet
- 1 (16-oz.) bag yellow candy wafers
- ½ bag (8 oz.) white candy wafers
- 2 silicone bowls or deep microwave-safe plastic bowls or cups
- paramount crystals
- black licorice string
- scissors
- 12 paper lollipop sticks
- 24 mini confetti sprinkles
- toothpicks
- Styrofoam block
- prepared piping bag containing dark chocolate candy coating
- prepared piping bag containing orange candy coating (advanced)

PREPARATION:

Using a cookie scoop, scoop cake pop dough and shape first into an oval. Then shape one end to be smaller, like a droplet shape, except both ends should be rounded. Place on a wax paper–lined cookie sheet. Chill in the refrigerator for 10–15 minutes.

While the dough chills, melt the yellow and white candy wafers separately in microwave in silicone bowls. Thin the consistency with paramount crystals if necessary and let rest at room temperature for at least 5 minutes before dipping.

With scissors, cut black licorice string into ½-inch pieces. There should be 24 pieces.

DECORATING:

Remove the dough shapes from the refrigerator and let rest at room temperature for a few minutes. Dip about ⅓ inch of one end of the lollipop stick into the candy coating and then, with the droplet-shaped cake ball at a 45-degree angle, insert the stick vertically and push into the middle about halfway.

Dip the edges of 2 mini confetti sprinkles into the candy coating and push into the top corners of the head (for the ears).

Once you've attached all the sticks and ears, refrigerate cae pops for 2–3 minutes to help harden the candy coating.

When you're ready to dip, hold the cake pop stick vertically, with the cake pop upside down. Dip into the yellow candy coating. Submerge completely and pull out. Lightly wiggle to allow the excess coating to slide off the top. Use a toothpick to pierce any air bubbles stuck in the coating or to guide excess candy coating off the cake pop.

Turn right side up and gently push 2 pieces of black licorice in the area between the ears. Place pops on a Styrofoam block and let dry completely. If you feel that the licorice pieces are too long, trim them carefully with sharp scissors.

Next, tilt the cake pop slightly forward and dip just the bottom large-portioned end of the cake pop into the white coating.

Using the prepared piping bag with dark chocolate candy coating, pipe two eyes and a smile onto each giraffe.

Advanced: Use the piping bag with orange candy coating to pipe a giraffe spot pattern on the backs of the heads.

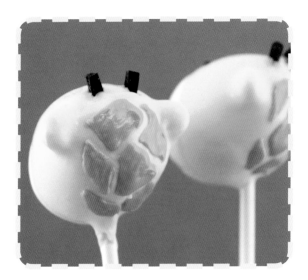

KRIS GALICIA BROWN

ELEPHANTS

You'll need:

- 12 uncoated round cake balls, chilled
- wax paper
- cookie sheet
- 16 oz. "soft charcoal" candy wafer mix (pg. 13)
- 24 white candy wafers
- silicone bowl, or a deep microwave-safe plastic bowl or cup
- paramount crystals
- small sharp knife
- 4 gummy worms
- toothpicks
- Styrofoam block
- 12 paper lollipop sticks
- prepared piping bag containing black candy coating
- prepared piping bag containing light pink candy coating

PREPARATION:

Using a cookie scoop, scoop and shape cake pop dough into balls. Place on a wax paper–lined cookie sheet. Chill in the refrigerator for 10–15 minutes.

While the dough chills, melt the "soft charcoal" candy wafer mix in the microwave in a silicone bowl. Thin the consistency with paramount crystals if necessary and let rest at room temperature for at least 5 minutes before dipping.

Using a small sharp knife, cut each gummy worm crosswise into 3 equal pieces. These will be the elephant trunks. The gummy worms also provide realistic ridges along the trunk. Choose gummy worms with twists and bends—they will make for more lively elephants!

CUSTOM CAKE POPS

Push one toothpick into the cut end of each gummy worm piece. Dip each piece into the "soft charcoal" candy coating, but only dip flush to the edge; do not submerge completely. Place on Styrofoam block and let dry completely. Once dry, slowly and carefully remove the toothpicks from the trunks.

DECORATING:

Remove the cake balls from the refrigerator. Let rest at room temperature for a few minutes. Dip about ⅓ inch of one end of the lollipop stick into the candy coating and then insert into the cake ball and push until the stick is about halfway through the ball.

Dip the edges of 2 wafers in candy coating and, with the flat side facing forward, push into each side of the uncoated cake pop. These will be the elephant ears.

Once you've attached all the sticks and ears, refrigerate cake pops for 2–3 minutes to help set and harden the candy coating.

When you're ready to dip, hold the cake pop stick vertically, with the cake pop upside down. Dip into candy coating. Submerge completely (being very careful because of the width) and pull out. Lightly wiggle to allow the excess coating to slide off the top. Use a toothpick to pierce any air bubbles stuck in the coating or to help guide excess candy coating off the cake pop. Place on the Styrofoam block and let dry completely.

Use a toothpick to dab candy coating on the middle of the face. Attach a trunk by placing the uncoated end (the side the toothpick was inserted) onto the face and hold in place until the coating sets.

Using a piping bag with black candy coating, pipe two small eyes.

Finally, using a piping bag with light pink candy coating, pipe a pink semicircle in each ear.

KRIS GALICIA BROWN

elephant

lion

KRIS GALICIA BROWN

LIONS

You'll need:

- 12 uncoated round cake balls, chilled
- wax paper
- cookie sheet
- 1 (16-oz.) bag yellow candy wafers

- silicone bowl, or a deep microwave-safe plastic bowl or cup
- paramount crystals
- toothpicks
- 120 round orange candy necklace pieces

- 12 paper lollipop sticks
- Styrofoam block
- prepared piping bag containing chocolate candy coating

PREPARATION:

Using a cookie scoop, scoop and shape cake pop dough into balls. Place on a wax paper–lined cookie sheet. Chill in the refrigerator for 10–15 minutes.

While the dough chills, melt the yellow candy wafers in the microwave in a silicone bowl. Thin the consistency with paramount crystals if necessary and let rest at room temperature for at least 5 minutes before dipping.

DECORATING:

Remove the cake balls from the refrigerator. Let rest at room temperature for a few minutes. Dip about ⅓ inch of one end of the lollipop stick into the candy coating and then, with the oval laying horizontally, insert stick into the middle and push until the stick is about halfway through the ball.

Once you've attached all the sticks, refrigerate for 2–3 minutes to help harden the candy coating.

When you're ready to dip, hold the cake pop stick vertically, with the cake pop upside down. Dip into yellow candy coating. Submerge completely and pull out. Lightly wiggle to allow the excess coating to slide off the top. Use a toothpick to pierce any air bubbles stuck in the coating or to guide excess candy coating off the cake pop.

Turn right side up and, while the coating is still wet, place 10 orange candy necklace pieces side by side around the cake pop, creating a mane. Place cake pops on a Styrofoam block to dry completely.

Finally, using a piping bag with chocolate candy coating, pipe two small eyes and a nose that descends into a line and a mouth.

FOXES

You'll need:

- 12 uncoated cake balls shaped like rounded rectangles, chilled
- wax paper
- cookie sheet
- 1 (16-oz.) bag super white candy wafers
- 8 oz. "fire burst" candy wafer mix (pg. 13)

- 2 silicone bowls or deep microwave-safe plastic bowls or cups
- paramount crystals
- 12 paper lollipop sticks
- 24 triangle sprinkles

- toothpicks
- Styrofoam block
- disposable glove
- prepared piping bag containing black candy coating

PREPARATION:

Using a cookie scoop, scoop and shape cake pop dough into rounded rectangles. Place on a wax paper–lined cookie sheet. Chill in the refrigerator for 10–15 minutes.

While the dough chills, melt the super white candy wafers and "fire burst" candy wafer mix separately in the microwave in silicone bowls. Thin the consistency with paramount crystals if necessary and let rest at room temperature for at least 5 minutes before dipping.

DECORATING:

Remove the rounded rectangular shapes from the refrigerator. Let rest at room temperature for a few minutes. Dip about ⅓ inch of one end of the lollipop stick into the candy coating and then insert stick into the middle of the wider side of the cake shape and push until the stick is about halfway through the shape

Dip the bases of 2 triangle sprinkles in candy coating and attach them on top of the head as far wide as you can place them (ears).

Once you've attached all the sticks and triangle ears, refrigerate cake pops for 2–3 minutes to help harden the candy coating.

When you're ready to dip, hold the cake pop stick vertically, with the cake pop upside down. Dip into super white candy coating. Submerge completely and pull out. Lightly wiggle to allow the excess coating to slide off the top. Use a toothpick to pierce any air bubbles stuck in the coating or to guide excess candy coating off the cake pop. Let dry on a Styrofoam block.

Put a disposable glove on your dominant hand. Hold the cake pop stick vertically with your non-dominant hand, with the cake pop upside down. Dip halfway into "fire burst" candy coating and pull out. Lightly wiggle to allow the excess coating to slide off the top.

Turn right side up. Using the thumb on your gloved hand, gently swipe off "fire burst" coating from the center out to each side, creating an upward bend on what was once a straight edge of coating. Wipe your glove clean between each swipe.

Use a toothpick to dab super white coating in the center of each ear.

Using a piping bag with black candy coating, pipe two small eyes and a nose at the point you created in the center from the swiping motions.

foxes

love birds

KRIS GALICIA BROWN

LOVE BIRDS

You'll need:

- 12 uncoated cake balls shaped into hearts, chilled
- wax paper
- cookie sheet
- 1 (16-oz.) bag red candy wafers
- silicone bowl, or a deep microwave-safe plastic bowl or cup
- paramount crystals
- 12 paper lollipop sticks
- toothpicks
- 36 jumbo heart sprinkles
- 24 (4mm) eye sprinkles
- 12 yellow rainbow chip sprinkles
- Styrofoam block

PREPARATION:

Using a cookie scoop, scoop and shape cake pop dough into hearts. The best way to do this is to shape the dough as a ball first and then place it in the middle of both hands with palms facing up. Using the outer side of your palms, slowly put pressure on the bottom of the round dough and rub your hands forward and backward simultaneously to create an upside-down droplet shape. Use your fingers to form the bottom point by lightly pinching the dough. To create the top portion of the heart, take a lollipop stick and push it down on the top middle area about ¼ inch. This creates the small divide. Use your fingers to round each of the two upper sides by pushing and pinching gently. Place on a wax paper–lined cookie sheet. Chill in the refrigerator for 10–15 minutes.

While the dough chills, melt the red candy wafers in the microwave in a silicone bowl. Thin the consistency with paramount crystals if necessary and let rest at room temperature for at least 5 minutes before dipping.

DECORATING:

Remove the heart shapes from the refrigerator. Let rest at room temperature for a few minutes. Dip about ⅓ inch of one end of the lollipop stick into the candy coating and then insert into the bottom of the heart until the stick is about halfway through.

Once you've attached all the sticks, refrigerate the cake pops for 2–3 minutes to harden the candy coating.

When you're ready to dip, hold the cake pop stick vertically, with the cake pop upside down. Dip into red candy coating. Submerge completely and pull out. Lightly wiggle to allow the excess coating to slide off the top. Use a toothpick to pierce any air bubbles stuck in the coating or to guide excess candy coating off the cake pop. Turn right side up.

With the coating still wet, attach jumbo hearts: Push one sideways into the left upper- and outermost area of the heart shape, creating a tail. Add one on each side of the front and back of the heart shape, creating wings.

Place an eye sprinkle on the front and back side, in the right upper quadrant.

Finally, add a yellow rainbow chip sprinkle on the right upper- and outermost area, creating the beak.

Place cake pops on a Styrofoam block and let dry completely.

KRIS GALICIA BROWN

OWLS

You'll need:

- 12 uncoated round cake balls, chilled
- wax paper
- cookie sheet
- 1 (16-oz.) bag light pink candy wafers
- silicone bowl, or a deep microwave-safe plastic bowl or cup
- paramount crystals
- small sharp knife
- 12 Mike and Ike candies
- 12 paper lollipop sticks
- 24 white chocolate chips
- toothpicks
- 24 (4mm) eye sprinkles
- Styrofoam block
- prepared piping bag containing orange candy coating
- prepared piping bag containing "Granny Smith" candy coating (pg. 13)

PREPARATION:

Using a cookie scoop, scoop and shape cake pop dough into balls. Place on a wax paper–lined cookie sheet. Chill in the refrigerator for 10–15 minutes.

While the dough chills, melt the light pink candy wafers in the microwave in a silicone bowl. Thin the consistency with paramount crystals if necessary and let rest at room temperature for at least 5 minutes before dipping.

Using a small sharp knife, cut each Mike and Ike candy diagonally in half lengthwise.

DECORATING:

Remove the balls from the refrigerator and let rest at room temperature for a few minutes. Dip about ⅓ inch of one end of the lollipop stick into the candy coating and then insert into the balls in the middle until the stick is halfway through.

Using a toothpick, dab candy coating on the top outer sides of the cake ball. Attach 2 chocolate chips to create ears. In the same manner, on both sides of the body just below the chocolate chip ears, attach 2 of the Mike and Ike candies, the cut side attached to the body. Make sure the thicker end of the candy piece is down. These will be the wings.

Once you've attached all the sticks, ears, and wings, refrigerate for 2–3 minutes to help harden the candy coating.

When you're ready to dip, hold the cake pop stick vertically, with the cake pop upside down. Dip into candy coating. Submerge completely and pull out. Lightly wiggle to allow the excess coating to slide off. Use a toothpick to pierce any air bubbles stuck in the coating or to guide excess candy coating off the cake pop. Turn right side up and continue to tap off the excess if necessary.

While still wet, place two eye sprinkles side by side on the top half of the cake pop just below the ears. Place on a Styrofoam block and let dry completely.

Using a piping bag with orange candy coating, pipe a small triangle beak under and between the eyes.

Finally, using a piping bag with "Granny Smith" candy coating, pipe a chevron (zigzag) pattern on the lower half of the owl cake pops.

KRIS GALICIA BROWN

owl

CUSTOM CAKE POPS

ravens

KRIS GALICIA BROWN

RAVENS

You'll need:

- 12 uncoated cake balls, shaped into round-edged wedges, chilled
- wax paper
- cookie sheet
- 16 oz. "dark night" candy wafer mix (pg. 13)
- silicone bowl, or a deep microwave-safe plastic bowl or cup
- paramount crystals
- small sharp knife
- 12 candy corns
- toothpicks
- Styrofoam block
- 12 paper lollipop sticks
- 12 cherry sours candies
- 24 (2mm) eye sprinkles

PREPARATION:

Using a cookie scoop, scoop and shape cake pop dough into round-edged wedges. Place on a wax paper–lined cookie sheet. Chill in the refrigerator for 10–15 minutes.

While the dough chills, melt the "dark night" candy wafer mix in the microwave in a silicone bowl. Thin the consistency with paramount crystals if necessary and let rest at room temperature for at least 5 minutes before dipping.

Using a sharp knife, cut the yellow portions off of the candy corns. Push one toothpick into the cut end of each candy corn. Dip each piece into the candy coating, but only dip to the edge—do not submerge completely.

Run a toothpick tip along the candy corn, from the center of the edge up and over to the other side and down to the edge. This creates the illusion of the separation of the beak. Place on Styrofoam block and let dry completely. Once dry, slowly and carefully remove the toothpicks from the candy corn.

DECORATING:

Remove the round-edged wedges from the refrigerator. Let rest at room temperature for a few minutes. Dip about ⅓ inch of one end of the lollipop stick into the candy coating and then, with the wedge pointing downward, insert the stick vertically into the middle from the bottom and push up until the stick is about halfway through the round-edged wedge (see photo on page 76 for stick placement).

Using candy coating as the "glue" to hold the shapes together, attach a cherry sour ball on top of the wedge.

Once you've attached all the sticks and cherry sours, refrigerate cake pops for 2–3 minutes to help harden the candy coating.

Dipping these cake pops will take a couple of steps. When you're ready to dip, hold the cake pop stick vertically, with the cake pop upside down.

Dip only the cherry sour (to the "neck") into the "dark night" candy coating. Lightly wiggle to allow the excess coating to slide off the top. Place on Styrofoam block and let dry completely.

Repeat this process another time, so the cherry sour head and neck area get two coatings. Place on Styrofoam block and let dry completely.

Next, dip the entire cake pop into the candy coating. Lightly wiggle to let the excess coating slide off.

Turn right side up and attach a beak and also two eye sprinkles, one on each side of the head.

Create some texture along the back of the bird by dipping a toothpick and then running it down in narrow "S" motions. Create an eyebrow above each eye as well by using a toothpick dipped in candy coating.

KRIS GALICIA BROWN

DUCKS

You'll need:

- 12 uncoated cake balls, each ball divided into 2 pieces in $1/3$ and $2/3$ portions, chilled
- wax paper
- cookie sheet
- 1 (16-oz.) bag yellow candy wafers
- silicone bowl, or a deep microwave-safe plastic bowl or cup
- paramount crystals
- small sharp knife
- 6 orange Starburst
- 12 paper lollipop sticks
- toothpicks
- 24 black sugar pearls
- Styrofoam block
- light blue sugar pearls (optional)

PREPARATION:

Using a cookie scoop, scoop dough portions. Split each portion by rolling $1/3$ of the portion into a ball and the remaining $2/3$ portion into a droplet. Repeat for every portion. Place on a wax paper–lined cookie sheet and chill in the refrigerator for 10–15 minutes.

While the dough chills, melt the yellow candy wafers in the microwave in a silicone bowl. Thin the consistency with paramount crystals if necessary and let rest at room temperature for at least 5 minutes before dipping.

Using a small sharp knife, cut each orange Starburst diagonally, totaling 12 triangular pieces. Using your fingers, mold Starburst triangles to resemble duck bills.

DECORATING:

Remove the small cake balls and drop-lets from the refrigerator. Let rest at room temperature for a few minutes. Dip about ⅓ inch of one end of the lollipop stick into the candy coating and then insert stick into the middle of the droplet from the bottom and push up until the stick is about halfway through the droplet.

Using candy coating as the "glue" to hold the shapes together, attach the smaller ball (head) to the top of the large portion of the droplet shape (body).

Once you've attached all the sticks and heads, re-frigerate for 2–3 minutes to help harden the candy coating.

When you're ready to dip, hold the cake pop stick vertically, with the cake pop upside down. Dip into yellow candy coating. Submerge completely and pull out. Lightly wiggle to allow the excess coating to slide off the top. Use a toothpick to pierce any air bubbles stuck in the coating or to help fill the neck crease with candy coating.

Turn right side up and, while the coating is still wet, place orange duck bill in the center of the head. Then attach the black pearl eyes to the head just above the bill. Place in Styrofoam block and let dry completely.

If you desire a rubber ducky look, place blue sugar pearls randomly around the bottom edge to simulate bubbles.

KRIS GALICIA BROWN

ducks

shark

KRIS GALICIA BROWN

SHARKS

You'll need:

- 12 uncoated cake balls shaped into long flat-bottomed droplets, chilled
- wax paper
- cookie sheet
- 16 oz. "soft charcoal" candy wafer mix (pg. 13)
- silicone bowl, or a deep microwave-safe plastic bowl or cup
- paramount crystals
- 21 white candy wafers
- 5/8-inch fondant cutter (smallest sized Wilton cutter from the 3-piece set, pg. 4)
- small sharp knife
- 12 paper lollipop sticks
- toothpicks
- Styrofoam block
- prepared piping bag containing black candy coating

PREPARATION:

Using a cookie scoop, scoop dough and form into flat-bottomed droplets. Place on a wax paper–lined cookie sheet and chill in the refrigerator for 10–15 minutes.

While the dough chills, melt the "soft charcoal" candy wafer mix in the microwave in a silicone bowl. Thin the consistency with paramount crystals if necessary and let rest at room temperature for at least 5 minutes before dipping.

Separate 12 of the white candy wafers to shape as the shark tail: line up the edge of a 5/8-inch cutter with the edge of the white wafer disc and cut into the wafer disc. Trim the ends and edges with the cutter until you've achieved a nice crescent shape.

Cut each of the remaining 9 white candy wafers

into fourths, using a sharp knife to make a vertical cut and then a horizontal cut down the center. You should have a total of 36 small triangular pieces.

These will make the side fins and dorsal fin of the sharks. Use the small cutter again to cut a detailed curve from one of the straight sides of the fins.

DECORATING:

Remove the flat-bottomed droplets from the refrigerator. Let rest at room temperature for a few minutes. Dip about ⅓ inch of one end of the lollipop stick into the candy coating and then, with the droplet horizontal, flat side down, insert stick into the middle from the bottom and push up until the stick is about halfway through the droplet.

Then attach the tail crescent by first positioning it through the pointed end of the droplet. Push it in, slightly splitting the pointed end. When you're satisfied with the positioning, dip a toothpick into candy coating and use to secure the tail fin in place.

Follow by attaching dorsal fin, dipping the fat edge into candy coating and pushing it into the center of the top, curved edge forward. Next, attach side fins in the same manner, curved edge forward.

Once you've attached all the sticks and fins, refrigerate cake pops for 2–3 minutes to help set and harden the candy coating.

When you're ready to dip, hold the cake pop stick vertically, with the cake pop upside down. Dip into candy coating. Submerge completely and pull out. Lightly wiggle to allow the excess coating to slide off the tail. Use a toothpick to pierce any air bubbles stuck in the coating or to help fill the neck crease with candy coating.

Turn right side up and place in Styrofoam block. Let dry completely.

Finally, use a piping bag with black candy coating to pipe two small oval eyes and a smile.

Advanced: Pipe a sharp-toothed smile.

KRIS GALICIA BROWN

MERMAID TAILS

You'll need:

- 12 uncoated cake balls shaped into mermaid tails, chilled
- small sharp knife
- 12 paper lollipop sticks
- wax paper
- cookie sheet
- 16 oz. "soft teal" candy wafer mix (pg. 13)
- silicone bowl, or a deep microwave-safe plastic bowl or cup
- paramount crystals
- toothpicks
- Styrofoam block
- prepared piping bag containing "soft teal" candy coating mix (pg. 13)
- prepared piping bag containing purple candy coating (advanced)
- prepared piping bag containing super white candy coating (advanced)

PREPARATION:

Shaping the mermaid tails will take a few steps. Using a cookie scoop, scoop and shape cake pop dough into a rectangle about 1 inch wide by 1½ inches tall. Then cut a lengthwise slit in the middle with a small knife, starting from the top edge, about ½ inch long. To shape each side, push and shape the dough outward, lightly pinching, shaping, and slightly elongating the dough. Create the pointed tip of the fin by pinching around the tip until a point is established. Repeat on the other side. Use a lollipop stick to help shape the center area where the two fins meet.

Next, shape the base of the tail by rounding off the edges, so it's less of a rectangle and more of an oval.

Using pressure from your fingertips and thumb, slightly fan out the base and make the area below the fins more slender. Place on a wax paper–lined cookie sheet. Chill in the refrigerator for 10–15 minutes.

While the dough chills, melt the "soft teal" candy wafer mix in the microwave in a silicone bowl. Thin the consistency with paramount crystals if necessary and let rest at room temperature for at least 5 minutes before dipping.

DECORATING:

Remove the mermaid tail shapes from the refrigerator. Let rest at room temperature for a few minutes. Dip about ⅓ inch of one end of the lollipop stick into the candy coating and then insert into the bottom (wide) edge of the tail until the stick is about halfway through.

Once you've attached all the sticks, refrigerate the cake pops for 2–3 minutes to help harden the candy coating.

When you're ready to dip, hold the cake pop stick vertically, with the cake pop upside down. Dip into "soft teal" candy coating. Submerge completely and pull out. Lightly wiggle to allow the excess coating to slide off the top. Use a toothpick to pierce any air bubbles stuck in the coating or to guide excess candy coating off the cake pop. Turn right side up and continue to tap the excess using the rim of your bowl. Place on a Styrofoam block.

Create scales on the mermaid tail using the prepared piping bag filled with "soft teal" coating. Pipe rows of semicircles around the base, starting from the bottom edge and tapering off into the center of the fins.

Advanced: Using a piping bag filled with purple candy coating, pipe lines on the fins that radiate from the tip onto the edges of the scales.

Finally, using a piping bag filled with super white coating, pipe waves on the bottom (wide) edge of the mermaid tails. The motion is like writing the letter "C" in cursive over and over.

Photo by Nicole Benitez Photography, for Paiges of Style

KRIS GALICIA BROWN

mermaid tails

starfish beach

KRIS GALICIA BROWN

STARFISH BEACH

You'll need:

- 12 uncoated round cake balls, chilled
- wax paper
- cookie sheet
- 1 (16-oz.) bag light blue candy wafers
- silicone bowl, or a deep microwave-safe plastic bowl or cup
- paramount crystals
- 12 paper lollipop sticks
- toothpicks
- toffee bits sprinkles
- Styrofoam block
- prepared piping bag containing red candy coating
- prepared piping bag containing orange candy coating
- prepared piping bag containing "Granny Smith" candy coating mix (pg. 13)
- prepared piping bag containing yellow candy coating

PREPARATION:

Using a cookie scoop, scoop and shape cake pop dough into balls. Place on a wax paper–lined cookie sheet. Chill in the refrigerator for 10–15 minutes.

While the dough chills, melt the light blue candy wafers in the microwave in a silicone bowl. Thin the consistency with paramount crystals if necessary and let rest at room temperature for at least 5 minutes before dipping.

DECORATING:

Remove the balls from the refrigerator and let rest at room temperature for a few minutes. Dip about ⅓ inch of one end of the lollipop stick into the candy coating and then insert sticks into the balls in the middle.

Once you've attached all the sticks, refrigerate cake pops for 2–3 minutes to help harden the candy coating.

When you're ready to dip, hold the cake pop stick vertically, with the cake pop upside down. Dip into light blue candy coating. Submerge completely and pull out. Lightly wiggle to allow the excess coating to slide off. Use a toothpick to pierce any air bubbles stuck in the coating or to guide excess candy coating off the cake pop. Turn right side up and continue to tap off the excess if necessary.

While the cake pop is still wet, hold it sideways and rotate it with your fingers while carefully adding toffee bits sprinkles on the bottom half. Place on a Styrofoam block and let dry completely.

Using a prepared piping bag, pipe one large starfish on the top of each cake pop. Pipe 3 each in red, orange, "Granny Smith," and yellow. Place on a Styrofoam block and let dry completely.

TIKI

You'll need:

- 12 uncoated cake balls shaped into wide cylinders, chilled
- wax paper
- cookie sheet
- 1 (16-oz.) bag chocolate candy wafers
- silicone bowl, or a deep microwave-safe plastic bowl or cup
- paramount crystals
- 12 paper lollipop sticks
- toothpicks
- Styrofoam block
- prepared piping bag containing chocolate candy coating with "fried tan" candy coating lightly swirled in (pg. 13)

PREPARATION:

Using a cookie scoop, scoop and shape cake pop dough into a cylinder. The best way to do this is to roll into an oval first and push the ends onto a flat surface and then gently roll on its side on your work surface. Place on a wax paper–lined cookie sheet and chill in the refrigerator for 10–15 minutes.

While the dough chills, melt the chocolate candy wafers in the microwave in a silicone bowl. Thin the consistency with paramount crystals if necessary and let rest at room temperature for at least 5 minutes before dipping.

DECORATING:

Remove the cylinder shapes from the refrigerator. Let rest at room temperature for a few minutes. Dip about ⅓ inch of one end of the lollipop stick into the candy coating and then insert into a flat end of the cylinder and push into the middle.

Once you've attached all the sticks, refrigerate cake pops for 2–3 minutes to help set the candy coating. Remove from the fridge.

When you're ready to dip, hold the cake pop stick vertically, with the cake pop upside down. Dip into chocolate candy coating. Submerge completely and pull out. Lightly wiggle to allow the excess coating to slide off the top edge. Use a toothpick to pierce any air bubbles stuck in the coating or to guide excess candy coating off the cake pop. Turn right side up, continue to tap off excess if necessary. Place on a Styrofoam block and let dry.

Using the piping bag filled with chocolate coating and "fried tan" coating swirl, pipe a small vertical line pattern along the top edge and bottom edge. Create a variety of faces in the center.

KRIS GALICIA BROWN

tiki

pineapple

KRIS GALICIA BROWN

PINEAPPLES

You'll need:

- 12 uncoated egg-shaped cake balls, chilled
- wax paper
- cookie sheet
- 1 (16-oz.) bag yellow candy wafers
- silicone bowl, or a deep microwave-safe plastic bowl or cup
- paramount crystals
- scissors
- 8 green gummy bears
- 12 paper lollipop sticks
- toothpicks
- Styrofoam block
- prepared piping bag containing green candy coating
- prepared piping bag containing "fried tan" candy coating (pg. 13)

PREPARATION:

Using a cookie scoop, scoop and shape cake pop dough into egg shapes. Place on a wax paper–lined cookie sheet and chill in the refrigerator for 10–15 minutes.

While the dough chills, melt the yellow candy wafers in the microwave in a silicone bowl. Thin the consistency with paramount crystals if necessary and let rest at room temperature for at least 5 minutes before dipping.

Using scissors, cut the green gummy bears into random long, thin triangular shapes.

DECORATING:

Remove the egg-shaped cake balls from the refrigerator. Let rest at room temperature for a few minutes. Dip about ⅓ inch of one end of the lollipop stick into the candy coating and then insert stick into the end of the oval and push into the middle.

Once you've attached all the sticks, refrigerate cake pops for 2–3 minutes to help set the candy coating. Remove from the fridge.

When you're ready to dip, hold the cake pop stick vertically, with the cake pop upside down. Dip into yellow candy coating. Submerge completely and pull out. Lightly wiggle to allow the excess coating to slide off the top edge. Use a toothpick to pierce any air bubbles stuck in the coating or to guide excess candy coating off the cake pop. Turn right side up and continue to tap off excess if necessary. Place on Styrofoam block and let dry completely.

To create the crown of the pineapple, use a prepared piping bag with green coating. Pipe a dollop of green coating on the center of the top and arrange cut gummy bear shapes on it with the points sticking up and out.

Use a prepared piping bag with "fried tan" coating and pipe the "eyes" of the pineapple: Create alternating rows of uniform semicircle shapes and dot the inside of each semicircle.

KRIS GALICIA BROWN

STRAWBERRIES

You'll need:

- 12 uncoated round-edged cone-shaped cake balls, chilled
- wax paper
- cookie sheet
- 1 (16-oz.) bag red candy wafers

- 2 oz. "Granny Smith" candy wafers
- 2 silicone bowls or deep microwave-safe plastic bowls or cups
- paramount crystals
- 4–6 mini pretzel rods
- 12 paper lollipop sticks

- toothpicks
- 72 green jumbo diamond sprinkles
- Styrofoam block
- prepared piping bag containing super white candy coating (advanced)

PREPARATION:

Using a cookie scoop, scoop and shape cake pop dough into a cone and round off the edge of the base, almost like a droplet shape but with the top-center area flattened. Place on a wax paper–lined cookie sheet. Chill in the refrigerator for 10–15 minutes.

While the dough chills, melt the red and "Granny Smith" candy wafers separately in the microwave in silicone bowls. Thin the consistency with paramount crystals if necessary and let rest at room temperature for at least 5 minutes before dipping.

Snap 4 mini pretzel rods into 3 pieces. If you want the appearance of long-stemmed strawberries, snap 6 mini pretzel rods in half.

Hold about ¼ inch of the pretzel rod pieces and dip each piece into the "Granny Smith" candy coating. Let dry on waxed paper.

DECORATING:

Remove the cone shapes from the refrigerator. Let rest at room temperature for a few minutes. Dip about ⅓ inch of one end of the lollipop stick into the candy coating and then insert stick into pointed end of the cone shape and push into the middle.

Once you've attached all the sticks, refrigerate cake pops for 2–3 minutes to help set the candy coating. Remove from the fridge.

Using one of the mini pretzel rod pieces, create an indentation on the top center of each cake pop.

When you're ready to dip, hold the cake pop stick vertically, with the cake pop upside down. Dip into candy coating. Submerge completely and pull out. Lightly wiggle to allow the excess coating to slide off the top edge. Use a toothpick to pierce any air bubbles stuck in the coating or to guide excess candy coating off the cake pop. Turn right side up and continue to tap off excess if necessary.

While the coating is still wet, place a mini coated pretzel rod piece, uncoated end down, into the indentation you made earlier. Carefully arrange 6 green jumbo diamond sprinkles around the pretzel "stem" in the center. Place on Styrofoam block and let dry completely.

Advanced: Using a piping bag with super white coating, pipe little dots in a uniform manner around each strawberry (for the seeds).

Photo by Melissa Biador Photography, for WED (weddings, events, design)

KRIS GALICIA BROWN

strawberries

banana

KRIS GALICIA BROWN

BANANAS

You'll need:

- 12 uncoated banana-shaped cake balls, chilled
- wax paper
- cookie sheet
- 1 (16-oz.) bag yellow candy wafers
- 4 oz. "Granny Smith" candy wafer mix (pg. 13)

- 2 silicone bowls or deep microwave-safe plastic bowls or cups
- paramount crystals
- 12 paper lollipop sticks
- 12 (½-inch) pieces Twizzlers Pull-n-Peel licorice

- toothpicks
- Styrofoam block
- prepared piping bag containing chocolate candy coating

PREPARATION:

Using a cookie scoop, scoop and shape cake pop dough into a banana shape, making sure the middle area is thicker than the ends. The best way to do this is to roll dough into an oval first and use your fingers to elongate and taper the ends into a crescent shape. Place on a wax paper–lined cookie sheet. Chill in the refrigerator for 10–15 minutes.

While the dough chills, melt the yellow wafers and "Granny Smith" wafer mix separately in the microwave in silicone bowls. Thin the consistency with paramount crystals if necessary and let rest at room temperature for at least 5 minutes before dipping.

DECORATING:

Remove the banana shapes from the refrigerator. Let rest at room temperature for a few minutes. Holding the crescents with the top end point straight up (more like an "L," rather than a "C"), find the center of gravity. Dip about ⅓ inch of one end of the lollipop stick into the candy coating and then insert stick into the bottom center and straight up from that area.

Dip one end of the licorice piece into candy coating and push it into the point of the banana. You want at least ¼ inch of the licorice piece to be visible. These are the stems.

Once you've attached all the sticks and stems, refrigerate cake pops for 2–3 minutes to help set the candy coating. Remove from the fridge.

When you're ready to dip, hold the cake pop stick vertically, with the cake pop upside down. Dip into yellow candy coating. Submerge completely and pull out. Lightly wiggle to allow the excess coating to slide off the top edge. Use a toothpick to pierce any air bubbles stuck in the coating or to guide excess candy coating off the cake pop. Turn right side up and continue to tap off excess if necessary.

While the coating is still wet, dip the top tip into the "Granny Smith" candy coating. Place on Styrofoam block and let dry completely.

Use the piping bag containing chocolate candy coating and dab a circle on the bottom tips of each banana.

KRIS GALICIA BROWN

POPSICLES

You'll need:

- 12 uncoated gravestone-shaped cake balls, chilled
- wax paper
- cookie sheet
- 1 (16-oz.) bag light pink candy wafers
- silicone bowl, or a deep microwave-safe plastic bowl or cup
- paramount crystals
- small sharp knife
- 12 mini wooden popsicle sticks
- toothpicks
- Styrofoam block
- small spoon

PREPARATION:

Using a cookie scoop, scoop and shape cake pop dough into gravestone shapes. Place on a wax paper–lined cookie sheet. Chill in the refrigerator for 10–15 minutes.

While the dough chills, melt the light pink candy wafers in the microwave in a silicone bowl. Thin the consistency with paramount crystals if necessary and let rest at room temperature for at least 5 minutes before dipping.

DECORATING:

Remove the gravestone shapes from the refrigerator and let rest at room temperature for a few minutes. Using a small knife, pierce up into the bottom of each gravestone in the middle. This will serve as a guide to place the popsicle sticks. Dip about ½ inch of one end of each mini wooden popsicle stick into the candy coating and then insert into the slits.

Once you've attached all the sticks, refrigerate the cake pops for 2–3 minutes to help harden the candy coating.

When you're ready to dip, hold the cake pop stick vertically, with the cake pop upside down. Dip into light pink candy coating. Submerge completely and pull out. Lightly wiggle to allow the excess coating to slide off the top. Use a toothpick to pierce any air bubbles stuck in the coating or to guide excess candy coating off the cake pop. Turn right side up and continue to tap off the excess if necessary and place on a Styrofoam block.

Use the tip of a small spoon to etch the lines that appear on the front and back of popsicles.

KRIS GALICIA BROWN

popsicle

ice cream cone

KRIS GALICIA BROWN

ICE CREAM CONES

You'll need:

- 12 uncoated cake balls, each split into three equal parts; shape into 12 cones and 24 balls, chilled
- wax paper
- cookie sheet
- 10 oz. "fried tan" candy wafer mix (pg. 13)
- 2/3 bag (about 10 oz.) purple candy wafers
- 2/3 bag (about 10 oz.) light pink candy wafers
- 3 silicone bowls or deep microwave-safe plastic bowls or cups
- paramount crystals
- 12 paper lollipop sticks
- toothpicks
- Styrofoam block
- rainbow jimmies
- prepared piping bag containing purple candy coating
- prepared piping bag containing light pink candy coating
- prepared piping bag containing "fried tan" candy coating (pg. 13)

PREPARATION:

Using a cookie scoop, scoop and split each cake ball into three equal parts, for a total of 36 smaller dough pieces. Shape 12 pieces into cones and 24 into balls, then place on a wax paper–lined cookie sheet. Chill in the refrigerator for 10–15 minutes.

While the dough chills, melt "fried tan," purple, and light pink candy wafers separately in the microwave in silicone bowls. Thin the consistency with paramount crystals if necessary and let rest at room temperature for at least 5 minutes before dipping.

DECORATING:

Remove the small cones and balls from the refrigerator. Let rest at room temperature for a few minutes.

Without dipping the lollipop sticks into candy coating, thread a cone onto each lollipop stick, inserting the stick into the pointed end of the cone and pushing it through until there's about 1½ inches of exposed stick above the flat side of the cone.

When you're ready to dip, hold the cake pop stick vertically, with the cone upside down. Dip into the "fried tan" candy coating. Submerge completely. Gently pull out and wiggle. Use a toothpick to pierce air bubbles trapped in the coating. Let as much of the excess drip off without letting the coating around the exposed tip of the stick harden. Then thread a cake ball through the stick and position it so it's almost touching the cone. Repeat the process with all 12 cake pops. A small portion of the tip of the stick should still be exposed. Let dry on a Styrofoam block.

Next, dip only the uncoated ball in purple candy coating. Be very careful with coating the ball. You don't want to get purple coating on the cone portion. Gently pull out and let as much of the excess drip off without letting the coating around the exposed tip of the stick harden. Then attach another small cake ball onto the stick so it's almost touching the purple coated cake ball. Repeat the process with all 12 cake pops and let dry on a Styrofoam block.

Repeat the dipping process into the light pink candy coating for the top cake ball, being careful not to get light pink candy coating on the purple-coated portion.

Sprinkle some rainbow jimmies over the top.

Advanced: Using the pink and purple prepared piping bags, pipe a little texture and melting drips on the base of each ball.

Finally, using the "fried tan" prepared piping bag, pipe dots in diagonal lines along the cone.

KRIS GALICIA BROWN

BARBECUE GRILLS

You'll need:

- 12 uncoated round cake balls, chilled
- wax paper
- cookie sheet
- 2/3 bag (about 10 oz.) red candy wafers
- 2/3 bag (about 10 oz.) yellow candy wafers
- 2/3 bag (about 10 oz.) light blue candy wafers
- 3 silicone bowls or deep microwave-safe plastic bowls or cups
- paramount crystals
- 36 (4-inch) paper lollipop sticks (or use trimmed 6-inch sticks)
- toothpicks
- electrical pliers
- small spoon
- prepared piping bag containing red candy coating
- prepared piping bag containing yellow candy coating
- prepared piping bag containing light blue candy coating
- prepared piping bag containing chocolate candy coating

PREPARATION:

Using a cookie scoop, scoop and shape cake pop dough into balls. Place on a wax paper–lined cookie sheet. Chill in the refrigerator for 10–15 minutes.

While the dough chills, melt the red, yellow, and light blue candy wafers separately in the microwave in silicone bowls. Thin the consistency with paramount crystals if necessary and let rest at room temperature for at least 5 minutes before dipping.

DECORATING:

Remove the balls from the refrigerator and let rest at room temperature for a few minutes. You will be inserting three sticks, each at an angle and equally spaced, into the bottom of each cake ball: Dip about ⅓ inch of one end of the lollipop stick into the candy coating and then insert into the ball at an angle, with each stick about ¼ inch from the center.

Once you've attached all the sticks, place cake pops on the cookie sheet upside down, with the sticks up in the air. Refrigerate them for 2–3 minutes to help harden the candy coating around the stick.

Remove cake pops from the fridge. Stand each cake pop on the three legs. Using electrical pliers, snip off small pieces of the legs so each grill cake pop stands balanced.

Four cake pops will be dipped into each color: Hold the cake pop upside down by the sticks. Dip into the candy coating. Submerge until the sticks meet the candy coating. Using the small spoon, spoon candy coating onto the bottom of the grill, in between the sticks. Lift out and lightly wiggle to allow the excess coating to slide off. Use a toothpick to pierce any air bubbles stuck in the coating or to guide excess candy coating off the cake pop. Turn right side up and continue to tap off the excess if necessary.

Using piping bags filled with red, yellow, and light blue candy coating, pipe a line around the center of each cake pop, like an equator. Using a piping bag containing chocolate candy coating, pipe a small line on the top of each grill for the handle.

Advanced: Create wheels by using a small button mold and the piping bags in red, yellow, and light blue. You'll need 2 wheels for each grill, coordinating the colors to match. Dip two sticks in coordinating color and attach a coordinating button wheel on the outside of each stick.

Photo by Sonny Sbranti, for Hostess with the Mostess

KRIS GALICIA BROWN

barbecue grill

sushi

KRIS GALICIA BROWN

SUSHI

You'll need:

- 12 uncoated cake balls shaped like short and wide cylinders, chilled
- wax paper
- cookie sheet
- 1 (16-oz.) bag super white candy wafers
- ½ (16-oz.) bag black candy wafers

- 2 silicone bowls or deep microwave-safe plastic bowls or cups
- paramount crystals
- scissors
- 16 gummy bears: 4 each in green, red, white, and yellow

- 12 paper lollipop sticks
- toothpicks
- white sugar pearls
- Styrofoam block
- butter knife
- chopsticks

PREPARATION:

Using a cookie scoop, scoop and shape cake pop dough into a cylinder, about ¾ inch in height. The best way to do this is to roll dough into an oval, push the ends onto a flat surface, and then gently roll on its side on your work surface. Place on a wax paper–lined cookie sheet. Chill in the refrigerator for 10–15 minutes.

While the dough chills, melt the super white and black candy wafers separately in the microwave in silicone bowls. Thin the consistency with paramount crystals if necessary and let rest at room temperature for at least 5 minutes before dipping.

Using scissors, cut each gummy bear into 3 pieces crosswise. Sort in groupings of 4, one piece in each color.

DECORATING:

Remove the cylinder shapes from the refrigerator. Let rest at room temperature for a few minutes. Dip about ⅓ inch of one end of the lollipop stick into the candy coating, then insert into a flat end of the cylinder, and push stick halfway through.

Once you've attached all the sticks, refrigerate cake pops for 2–3 minutes to help set the candy coating. Remove from the fridge.

When you're ready to dip, hold the cake pop stick vertically, with the cake pop upside down. Dip into super white candy coating. Submerge completely and pull out. Lightly wiggle to allow the excess coating to slide off the top edge. Use a toothpick to pierce any air bubbles stuck in the coating or to guide excess candy coating off the cake pop. Turn right side up and continue to tap off excess coating if necessary.

Work quickly while the coating is still wet: place and arrange the 4 pieces of gummy bears flat in the center. Then carefully place the white sugar pearls, covering the entire top area of the cake pop surrounding the gummy bears. Place on Styrofoam block to dry.

Using a butter knife, spread the black candy coating around the side of the cake pop. Work slowly and carefully, making sure not to get any black coating on the top area. If the black candy coating isn't thick enough to spread, let it sit and firm up before spreading.

Use chopsticks to display the cake pop. Carefully remove the lollipop stick by gently twisting it out. Fill the hole with candy coating. Spread some black coating on the sides and "glue" the chopsticks to the sushi cake pop.

DONUTS

You'll need:

- 12 uncoated cake balls shaped like donuts, chilled
- jumbo plastic straw or souvenir straw
- wax paper
- cookie sheet
- 16 oz. "fried tan" candy wafer mix
- ½ (16-oz.) bag light pink candy wafers
- 2 silicone bowls or deep microwave-safe plastic bowls or cups
- paramount crystals
- toothpicks
- 12 plastic mini cocktail forks
- Styrofoam block
- rainbow jimmies

PREPARATION:

Using a cookie scoop, scoop and shape cake pop dough into donuts with the aid of a jumbo plastic straw (those that come with souvenir cups work perfectly): on your work surface, disperse and shape the dough evenly around the jumbo straw. Push gently from the side inward all the way around to puff up the top. Remove the straw and, using your fingers, smooth and round any edges made by the initial shaping. Place on a wax paper–lined cookie sheet. Chill in the refrigerator for 10–15 minutes.

While the dough chills, melt "fried tan" and light pink candy wafers separately in the microwave in silicone bowls. Thin the consistency with paramount crystals if necessary and let rest at room temperature for at least 5 minutes before dipping.

If there is a break in the dough within the donut shape, dab candy coating in that area with a toothpick and use your fingers to smooth it out. This will help "glue" it together.

DECORATING:

Remove the donut shapes from the refrigerator. Let rest at room temperature for a few minutes. Dip about ¼ inch of the mini cocktail fork prongs into the "fried tan" candy coating and then insert into the side of the donut.

Once you've attached all the mini cocktail forks, refrigerate cake pops for 2–3 minutes to help harden the candy coating.

Dip into "fried tan" candy coating. Submerge completely and pull out. Lightly wiggle to allow the excess coating to slide off. Use a toothpick to pierce any air bubbles stuck in the coating or to guide excess candy coating off the cake pop. Turn right side up and continue to tap the excess using the rim of your bowl. Place on a Styrofoam block to dry.

Line your work surface with a piece of wax paper. Tilt the bowl containing the pink candy coating slightly so it becomes easier to dip. Dip only the top half of the donut and lay the donut down, pink side up, on the wax paper. Sprinkle with rainbow jimmies.

KRIS GALICIA BROWN

donut

hot cocoa mug

KRIS GALICIA BROWN

HOT COCOA MUGS

You'll need:

- 12 uncoated cake balls shaped like cylinders, chilled
- wax paper
- cookie sheet
- 1 (16-oz.) bag super white candy wafers

- silicone bowl, or a deep microwave-safe plastic bowl or cup
- paramount crystals
- 12 paper lollipop sticks
- 12 (1½-inch) pieces Twizzlers Pull-n-Peel licorice
- toothpicks

- Styrofoam block
- prepared piping bag containing chocolate candy coating
- prepared piping bag containing "fried tan" candy coating (pg. 13)

PREPARATION:

Using a cookie scoop, scoop and shape cake pop dough into a cylinder. The best way to do this is to roll into an oval, push the ends onto a flat surface, and then gently roll on its side on your work surface. Place on a wax paper–lined cookie sheet. Chill in the refrigerator for 10–15 minutes.

While the dough chills, melt the super white candy wafers in the microwave in a silicone bowl. Thin the consistency with paramount crystals if necessary and let rest at room temperature for at least 5 minutes before dipping.

DECORATING:

Remove the cylinder shapes from the refrigerator. Let rest at room temperature for a few minutes. Dip about ⅓ inch of one end of the lollipop stick into the candy coating and then insert into a flat end of the cylinder and push about halfway through.

Once you've attached all the sticks, refrigerate the cake pops for 2–3 minutes to help set the candy coating. Remove from the fridge. On one side of the cylinder, create indentations using the ends of a Twizzler piece—this will make your handle. Once you're satisfied with the location of the handle, dip the edges of the licorice into the candy coating and insert handle into your indentations.

When you're ready to dip, hold the cake pop stick vertically, with the cake pop upside down. The licorice is flexible, but try not to push it against the wall of the bowl. Dip cake pops into candy coating. Submerge completely and pull out. Lightly wiggle to allow the excess coating to slide off the top edge. Use a toothpick to pierce any air bubbles stuck in the coating or to guide excess candy coating off the cake pop. You'll notice a thin film of coating within the handle's empty space. Use a toothpick to break this film. Turn right side up and continue to tap off excess if necessary. Place on Styrofoam block to dry.

Using the piping bag filled with chocolate candy coating, pipe a wide circle on the top of the mug and fill it with the candy coating to create the illusion that there's hot cocoa in the mug. Use a toothpick to disperse the chocolate coating within the area if necessary.

Using the piping bag filled with "fried tan" candy coating mixture, pipe a loose swirl on top of the chocolate coating.

Advanced: Use a toothpick to etch the words *HOT COCOA* on the side of the mug. Then using the piping bag with chocolate coating, pipe over your etching.

KRIS GALICIA BROWN

TEACUPS

You'll need:

- 12 uncoated cake balls shaped like bells, chilled
- wax paper
- cookie sheet
- 1 (16-oz.) bag super white candy wafers
- silicone bowl, or a deep microwave-safe plastic bowl or cup
- paramount crystals

- skewer
- 12 super white candy wafers
- 12 paper lollipop sticks
- 12 (1½-inch) pieces Twizzlers Pull-n-Peel licorice
- toothpicks
- Styrofoam block
- prepared piping bag containing light pink candy coating

Advanced:

- 3 pink Starburst
- rolling pin
- small knife
- prepared piping bag containing green candy coating
- prepared piping bag containing super white candy coating
- sugar crystals
- gold luster dust (optional)

PREPARATION:

Using a cookie scoop, scoop and shape cake pop dough into bells. The best way to do this is to roll dough into an oval, push onto a flat surface, and use your thumb and index fingers to help the edges of the dough meet the flat surface. Then gently curve out the body. Make sure it's nice and even all the way around. Place on a wax paper–lined cookie sheet. Chill in the refrigerator for 10–15 minutes.

While the dough chills, melt the super white candy wafers in the microwave in a silicone bowl. Thin the consistency with paramount crystals if necessary and let rest at room temperature for at least 5 minutes before dipping.

Using a skewer, carefully create a hole through the center of 12 super white candy wafers. This preps them for attachment. These wafers will be the "foot" of the teacups.

DECORATING:

Remove the bell shapes from the refrigerator. Let rest at room temperature for a few minutes. Dip about ⅓ inches of one end of the lollipop stick into the candy coating and then insert into the rounded part of the bell and push stick about halfway through.

Once you've attached all the sticks, refrigerate the cake pops for 2–3 minutes to help set the candy coating. Remove from the fridge. On one side of the teacup, create indentations using the ends of a Twizzler piece—this will make your handle. Once you're satisfied with the location of the handle, dip the edges of the licorice into the candy melts and insert into your indentations.

Place a pierced candy wafer flat side down and gently press and work the lollipop stick into it. Thread the wafer through the stick. For now, don't push the wafer all the way up—keep it about 2 inches from the uncoated cake pop.

When you're ready to dip, hold the cake pop stick vertically, with the cake pop upside down. The licorice is flexible, but try not to push it against the wall of the bowl. Dip into candy coating. Submerge completely and pull out. Lightly wiggle to allow the excess coating to slide off the top edge. Use a toothpick to pierce any air bubbles stuck in the coating or to guide excess candy coating off the cake pop. You'll notice a thin film of coating within the handle's empty space. Use a toothpick to break this film. Turn right side up and tap off excess if necessary. Slide the wafer up and position it so it touches the bottom of the teacup. The candy coating will help keep it in place. Place on Styrofoam block to dry.

Use a piping bag with light pink coating to create a lace-type pattern along the rim or top edge of the teacup.

Advanced: Unwrap each pink Starburst and flatten using a rolling pin. Cut four strips from each flattened Starburst. Create rosettes using these strips by rolling them tightly and then slightly pinching the bottom of the rosettes to give them more of a bloomed shape.

Pipe three dots of pink candy coating in the center of a teacup. Attach three rosettes to the center on top of the piped candy coating dots. Using the piping bag filled with green candy coating, pipe leaves around the rosettes.

Using the piping bag with super white coating, pipe coating around the top edge of the teacup and sprinkle with sugar crystals.

If desired, brush the handle and along the sugar crystals with gold luster dust.

KRIS GALICIA BROWN

teacup

hearts

KRIS GALICIA BROWN

HEARTS

You'll need:

- 12 uncoated cake balls shaped like hearts, chilled
- wax paper
- cookie sheet
- 1 (16-oz.) bag light pink candy wafers

- silicone bowl, or a deep microwave-safe plastic bowl or cup
- paramount crystals
- 12 paper lollipop sticks
- toothpicks
- Styrofoam block

- prepared piping bag containing light pink candy coating

Advanced:

- 8 mini pretzel sticks
- white (clear) sugar crystal sprinkles
- 36 jumbo red heart sprinkles

PREPARATION:

Using a cookie scoop, scoop and shape cake pop dough into hearts. The best way to do this is to shape the dough as a ball first and then place in the middle of both hands with palms facing up. Using the outer side of your palms, slowly put pressure on the bottom of the round dough and rub your hands forward and backward to create an upside down droplet shape. Use your fingers to form the bottom point by lightly pinching the dough. To create the top portion of the heart, take a lollipop stick and push it down on the top-middle area. Use your fingers to round the two upper sides by pushing and pinching gently. Place on a wax paper–lined cookie sheet. Chill in the refrigerator for 10–15 minutes.

While the dough chills, melt the light pink candy wafers in the microwave in a silicone bowl. Thin the consistency of candy coating with paramount crystals if necessary and let rest at room temperature for at least 5 minutes before dipping.

DECORATING:

Remove the heart shapes from the refrigerator. Let rest at room temperature for a few minutes. Dip about ⅓ inch of one end of the lollipop stick into the candy coating and then insert into the bottom of the heart until the stick is about halfway through.

Once you've attached all the sticks, refrigerate the cake pops for 2–3 minutes to help harden the candy coating.

When you're ready to dip, hold the cake pop stick vertically, with the cake pop upside down. Dip into light pink candy coating. Submerge completely and pull out. Lightly wiggle to allow the excess coating to slide off the top. Use a toothpick to pierce any air bubbles stuck in the coating or to help guide candy coating off the cake pop. Turn right side up and continue to tap the excess using the rim of your bowl. Place on a Styrofoam block to dry.

Using a piping bag filled with light pink coating, pipe messages like "Love" or other simple designs like swirls or a drizzle on the coated hearts.

Advanced: Instead of piping messages, snap each pretzel into 3 equal pieces. Before the coating hardens, attach a pretzel stick on one shoulder of the heart and the other at the bottom of the opposite side. This gives the illusion it's one piece that goes through the heart. Sprinkle the heart completely with sugar crystals. Attach jumbo heart sprinkles, using candy coating, on both ends of the pretzels.

KRIS GALICIA BROWN

MOLARS

You'll need:

- 12 uncoated cake balls shaped like cubes, chilled
- 12 paper lollipop sticks
- wax paper
- cookie sheet
- 1 (16-oz.) bag super white candy wafers
- silicone bowl, or a deep microwave-safe plastic bowl or cup
- paramount crystals
- small knife
- 48 candy corns
- toothpicks
- Styrofoam block

PREPARATION:

Using a cookie scoop, scoop and shape cake pop dough into cubes. Using a lollipop stick, make deep grooves on one side of the cube—the grooves will look a plus sign, or like there are four even squares on the surface. This surface will be the top of the tooth. Place on a wax paper–lined cookie sheet. Chill in the refrigerator for 10–15 minutes.

While the dough chills, melt the super white candy wafers in the microwave in a silicone bowl. Thin the consistency with paramount crystals if necessary and let rest at room temperature for at least 5 minutes before dipping.

Using a small knife, cut the yellow portions off 48 candy corns.

DECORATING:

Remove the cube shapes from the refrigerator and arrange them groove side down. Let rest at room temperature for a few minutes. Dip about ⅓ inch of one end of the lollipop stick into the candy coating and then insert the stick into the cubes, pushing about halfway through.

Using candy coating as "glue," attach a candy corn on each corner of the cube at a diagonal.

Once you've attached all the sticks and candy corn, refrigerate the cake pops for 2–3 minutes to help harden the candy coating.

When you're ready to dip, hold the cake pop stick vertically, with the cake pop upside down. Dip into super white candy coating. Submerge completely and pull out. Lightly wiggle to allow the excess coating to slide off the top. Turn right side up. You may need a toothpick to pierce air bubbles in the coating or to guide the excess candy coating into the grooves. Continue to tap off the excess if necessary and place on a Styrofoam block.

KRIS GALICIA BROWN

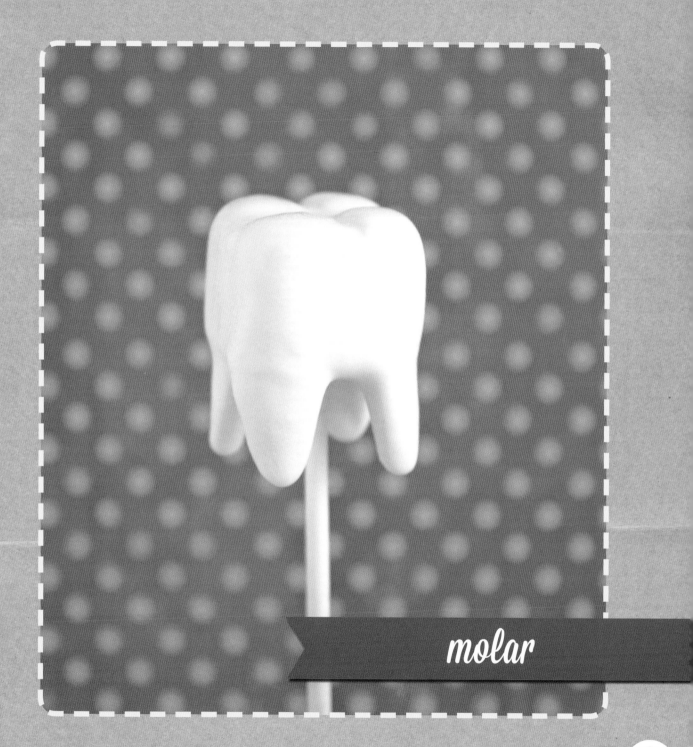

molar

hot air balloons

KRIS GALICIA BROWN

HOT AIR BALLOONS

You'll need:

- 12 uncoated cake balls shaped like droplets, chilled
- wax paper
- cookie sheet
- $\frac{2}{3}$ bag (about 10 oz.) red candy wafers
- $\frac{2}{3}$ bag (about 10 oz.) light blue candy wafers
- $\frac{2}{3}$ bag (about 10 oz.) yellow candy wafers
- $\frac{1}{2}$ (16-oz.) bag orange candy wafers
- $\frac{1}{2}$ (16-oz.) bag purple candy wafers
- $\frac{1}{2}$ (16-oz.) bag pink candy wafers

- 8 oz. "Granny Smith" candy wafers (pg. 13)
- 7 silicone bowls or deep microwave-safe plastic bowls or cups
- paramount crystals
- skewer
- 12 mini white (or chocolate) peanut butter cups
- 12 paper lollipop sticks
- toothpicks
- Styrofoam block
- prepared piping bag containing super white candy coating

Advanced:

- white sugar pearls
- prepared piping bag containing orange candy coating
- prepared piping bag containing light blue candy coating
- prepared piping bag containing purple candy coating
- prepared piping bag containing yellow candy coating
- prepared piping bag containing pink candy coating
- prepared piping bag containing "Granny Smith" candy coating (pg. 13)

PREPARATION:

Using a cookie scoop, scoop and shape cake pop dough into flat-bottomed droplets: Shape the dough as a ball first and then place in the middle of both hands with palms facing up. Slowly put pressure on the bottom of the dough and rub your hands forward and backward simultaneously to create an upside down droplet shape. Gently press the pointed end onto a flat surface. Place on a wax paper–lined cookie sheet. Chill in the refrigerator for 10–15 minutes.

While the dough chills, melt each color of candy wafers separately in the microwave in silicone bowls. Thin the consistency with paramount crystals if necessary and let rest at room temperature for at least 5 minutes before dipping. With a skewer, create holes through the center of each peanut butter cup. This preps them for attachment.

DECORATING:

Remove the dough shapes from the refrigerator. Let rest at room temperature for a few minutes. Dip about ⅓ inch of one end of the lollipop stick into the candy coating and then insert into the point of the droplet until the stick is about halfway through.

Once you've attached all the sticks, refrigerate the cake pops for 2–3 minutes to help harden the candy coating.

When you're ready to dip, hold the cake pop stick vertically, with the cake pop upside down. Dip cake pop into red candy coating. Submerge completely and pull out. Lightly wiggle to allow the excess coating to slide off the top. Use a toothpick to pierce any air bubbles stuck in the coating or to guide excess candy coating off the cake pop. Turn right side up and continue to tap the excess using the rim of your bowl. Place on a Styrofoam block.

Repeat with dipping a total of 4 cake pops into the red candy coating, 4 cake pops into light blue candy coating, and 4 cake pops into yellow candy coating. Let all dry on a Styrofoam block.

Start the next step with the red-dipped cake pops. Holding the cake pop upside down, dip ⅔ of the cake pop into the light blue coating and then rock the cake pop stick (only the stick) forward, back, left, and right. The rocking motion creates the curved- or scalloped-edged layers. Pull out and wiggle excess coating off while still upside down. Let dry on the Styrofoam block. Repeat with the other three red cake pops.

Once done with the blue-on-red combination, dip the light blue cake pops ⅔ of the way into the yellow coating. Rock the stick forward, back, left, and right. Once done with the yellow on light blue combo, move on to the next four cake pops. Dip

KRIS GALICIA BROWN

the solid yellow cake pops into the "Granny Smith" candy coating mixture using the same technique.

Once all twelve cake pops have 2 color layers on them, you can add the third layer. Start with the blue-on-red cake pops. Hold the cake pop upside down and position it so the curves will line up. Dip ⅓ of the cake pop into the orange and then rock the cake pop stick forward, back, left, and right, and then pull out, wiggle excess off while still upside down. Let dry on the Styrofoam block.

Repeat this process with the yellow-on-blue cake pops, dipping them into purple candy coating. And repeat the process again with the green-on-yellow cake pops, dipping them into pink candy coating. Let dry on a Styrofoam block.

Push white peanut butter cups up from the bottom of the stick. When you're happy with the position of the peanut butter cup, pipe super white coating where the peanut butter cup and lollipop stick meet.

Once the coating on all 12 cake pops has hardened, using the super white prepared piping bag, pipe four vertical lines on each cake pop, starting from where the rounded edges intersect (the point between each scalloped edge), down to the stick.

Advanced: Place white sugar pearls on top of the white line on the intersection points of each layer. There are 8 points on each cake pop.

Once the pearls are attached, still using the super white piping bag, pipe a bow to adorn each of the four pearls on the top row. Piping the bows is pretty simple if you think of it as writing a capital "R" without the vertical line on the right of the pearl, and doing the same on the left side of the pearl but with a mirror-image "R."

Once the lines are piped, the pearls are attached, and the bows are made on all the cake pops, define each scalloped edge using the prepared piping bags with coordinating colors.

Photo by Heart and Country, for Paiges of Style

bird nest

KRIS GALICIA BROWN

BIRD NESTS

You'll need:

- 12 uncoated cake balls shaped like domes, chilled
- wax paper
- cookie sheet
- 1 (16-oz.) bag chocolate candy wafers
- silicone bowl, or a deep microwave-safe plastic bowl or cup
- paramount crystals
- 12 paper lollipop sticks
- 36 Cadbury mini chocolate eggs or large jelly beans
- toothpicks
- Styrofoam block
- prepared piping bag containing melted chocolate candy coating

PREPARATION:

Using a cookie scoop, scoop and shape cake pop dough into domes. The best way to do this is to roll dough into a ball first and push onto a flat surface. Use your thumb and index fingers to help the edges of the dough meet the surface. Then gently shape the rounded dome so it's even all the way around. Place on a wax paper–lined cookie sheet. Chill in the refrigerator for 10–15 minutes.

While the dough chills, melt the chocolate candy wafers in the microwave in a silicone bowl. Thin the consistency with paramount crystals if necessary and let rest at room temperature for at least 5 minutes before dipping.

DECORATING:

Remove the domes from the refrigerator. Let rest at room temperature for a few minutes. Dip about ⅓ inch of one end of the lollipop stick into the candy coating and then insert into the rounded part of the dome and push about halfway through.

Once you've attached all the sticks to the domes, refrigerate the cake pops for 2–3 minutes to help set the candy coating. Remove from the fridge and, using a chocolate egg or jelly bean, make three small indentations on the flat part of the dome. This serves as a guide for placing the eggs or jelly beans after coating and will help keep them upright in the wet coating.

When you're ready to dip, hold the cake pop stick vertically, with the cake pop upside down. Dip into chocolate candy coating. Submerge completely and pull out. Lightly wiggle to allow the excess coating to slide off the top edge. Use a toothpick to pierce any air bubbles stuck in the coating or to guide candy coating off the cake pop. Turn right side up and tap off excess coating if necessary. Attach three

eggs or jelly beans in the center. Place on a Styrofoam block to dry

Using the piping bag with melted chocolate candy coating, pipe lines around the base of the nest. You'll need to pause for a moment to let the piping dry when you notice the drizzle lines are merging. Wait until they're set to pipe more layers of drizzled lines. This creates the texture of a woven nest.

Advanced: After piping lines around the nest, let the cake pop dry. Lay a piece of wax paper on your work surface. Using the piping bag filled with chocolate coating, drizzle squiggly lines up and down the waxed paper and let dry. Once these lines are dry, fold and bend the wax paper so the lines get broken up into small pieces.

On each cake pop, pipe some candy coating on the top area around the rim and between the eggs especially. Then sprinkle the small coating bits on the wet areas to make a realistic-looking, woven, twiggy nest.

EASTER BASKETS

You'll need:

- 12 uncoated cake balls shaped like domes, chilled
- wax paper
- cookie sheet
- 1 (16-oz.) bag chocolate candy wafers
- silicone bowl, or a deep microwave-safe plastic bowl or cup
- paramount crystals
- 12 paper lollipop sticks
- 12 (3½-inch) pieces Twizzlers Pull-n-Peel licorice
- 36 Cadbury mini chocolate eggs or jelly beans in different sizes and colors
- toothpicks
- Styrofoam block
- green jimmies
- prepared piping bag containing chocolate candy coating (advanced)

PREPARATION:

Using a cookie scoop, scoop and shape cake pop dough into domes. The best way to do this is to roll into a ball first and push onto a flat surface. Use your thumb and index fingers to help the edges of the dough meet the surface. Then gently shape the rounded dome so it's nice and even all the way around. Place on a wax paper–lined cookie sheet. Chill in the refrigerator for 10–15 minutes.

While the dough chills, melt the chocolate candy wafers in the microwave in a silicone bowl. Thin the consistency with paramount crystals if necessary and let rest at room temperature for at least 5 minutes before dipping.

DECORATING:

Remove the domes from the refrigerator. Let rest at room temperature for a few minutes. Dip about ⅓ inch of one end of the lollipop stick into the candy coating, insert into the rounded part of the dome, and push stick about halfway through.

Once you've attached all the sticks to the domes, refrigerate the cake pops for 2–3 minutes to help set the candy coating. Remove from the fridge and, using a chocolate egg or jelly bean, make three small indentations on the flat part of the dome. This serves as a guide for placing the eggs or jelly beans after coating and will also help keep them upright in the wet coating.

Using the ends of a Twizzler piece, create indentations in the flat part of the dough—this will make your basket handle. Try positioning the indentations across from each other as close to the edge as possible. Once you're satisfied with the location of the handle, dip the edges of the licorice into the candy melts and insert into your indentations.

When you're ready to dip, hold the cake pop stick vertically, with the cake pop upside down. The licorice is flexible, but try to bend it as little as possible. Dip cake pop into chocolate candy coating. Submerge completely and pull out. Lightly wiggle to allow the excess coating to slide off the top edge. Use a toothpick to pierce any air bubbles stuck in the coating or to guide candy coating off the cake pop. You'll notice the empty area within the basket handle will have a thin film of chocolate. Use a toothpick to break this film. Turn cake pop right side up and tap off excess coating if necessary. Attach three eggs or jelly beans in the center. Place on a Styrofoam block to dry.

With a toothpick, carefully add candy coating to the top of the basket around the eggs. Sprinkle with green jimmies to give the look of grass.

Dot more candy coating in areas that are lacking some "grass" and sprinkle with more green jimmies as needed.

Advanced: For a woven basket texture, use the prepared piping bag to pipe horizontal and vertical lines all the way around the basket.

KRIS GALICIA BROWN

Easter basket

brooms

KRIS GALICIA BROWN

BROOMS

You'll need:

- 12 uncoated cake balls shaped like pyramids with rectangular bases, chilled
- wax paper
- cookie sheet
- 1 (16-oz.) bag yellow candy wafers
- silicone bowl, or a deep microwave-safe plastic bowl or cup
- paramount crystals
- 12 mini pretzel sticks
- toothpicks
- prepared piping bag containing chocolate candy coating
- prepared piping bag containing black candy coating

PREPARATION:

Using a cookie scoop, scoop and shape cake pop dough into a wide cone and then press the sides against a flat surface to create a pyramid with a rectangular base. Place on a wax paper–lined cookie sheet. Chill in the refrigerator for 10–15 minutes.

While the dough chills, melt the yellow candy wafers in the microwave in a silicone bowl. Thin the consistency with paramount crystals if necessary and let rest at room temperature for at least 5 minutes before dipping.

DECORATING:

Remove the rectangular pyramid shapes from the refrigerator. Let rest at room temperature for a few minutes. Dip about ¼ inch of one end of a mini pretzel stick into the candy coating and then gently insert into the point of the pyramid, pushing down until the pretzel rod is about halfway through.

Once you've attached all the pretzel sticks, refrigerate the cake pops for 2–3 minutes to help harden the candy coating.

When you're ready to dip, hold the pretzel stick vertically and dip cake pop into yellow candy coating. Submerge completely and pull out. Gently wiggle to allow the excess coating to slide off. Use a toothpick to pierce any air bubbles stuck in the coating or to guide candy coating off the cake pop. Place on wax paper and let dry. Repeat for each broom.

Hold a broom by the pretzel stick. Using the piping bag with chocolate candy coating, pipe continuously in an up and down motion around the pyramid, waiting for each layer to dry before applying the next—this creates the broom's bristles. Continue to cover until not much yellow is visible.

Using the piping bag with black candy coating, pipe a black ring around the area where the pyramid and pretzel meet.

KRIS GALICIA BROWN

ROASTED TURKEYS

You'll need:

- 12 uncoated cake balls shaped like slight droplets, chilled
- 2 uncoated cake balls, each divided into 12 small portions (24 total) and shaped like droplets, chilled

- wax paper
- cookie sheet
- 16 oz. "roasted hazelnut" candy wafer mix (pg. 13)
- silicone bowl, or a deep microwave-safe plastic bowl or cup

- paramount crystals
- 12 paper lollipop sticks
- toothpicks
- 24 mini bone sprinkles
- Styrofoam block

PREPARATION:

Using a cookie scoop, scoop cake pop dough and shape first into an oval. Then shape one end to be smaller, like a slight droplet. Shape 24 separate pieces into small droplets. Place on a wax paper–lined cookie sheet. Chill in the refrigerator for 10–15 minutes.

While the dough chills, melt the "roasted hazelnut" candy wafer mix in the microwave in a silicone bowl. Thin the consistency with paramount crystals if necessary and let rest at room temperature for at least 5 minutes before dipping.

DECORATING:

Remove the shapes from the refrigerator and let rest at room temperature for a few minutes. Dip about ⅓ inch of one end of the lollipop stick into the candy coating, insert into the bottom of the droplet-shaped turkey body, and push stick about halfway through.

Using the candy coating as "glue," attach 2 mini droplets horizontally on each side of the narrower end of the turkey body, with the pointed ends facing outward—these are the turkey legs.

Once you've attached all the sticks and legs, refrigerate the cake pops for 2–3 minutes to help harden the candy coating.

When you're ready to dip, hold the cake pop stick vertically, with the cake pop upside down. Dip into the "roasted hazelnut" candy coating. Submerge completely and pull out. Lightly wiggle to allow the excess coating to slide off the legs and back end of the turkey. Use a toothpick to pierce any air bubbles stuck in the coating or to guide excess candy coating off the cake pop. Turn right side up and gently push a mini bone sprinkle into each pointed end of the turkey leg. Place cake pops on a Styrofoam block and let dry completely.

KRIS GALICIA BROWN

roasted turkey

CUSTOM CAKE POPS

mitten

KRIS GALICIA BROWN

MITTENS

You'll need:

- 12 uncoated cake balls shaped like enclosed horseshoes, chilled
- wax paper
- cookie sheet
- 1 (16-oz.) bag super white candy wafers

- silicone bowl, or a deep microwave-safe plastic bowl or cup
- paramount crystals
- 6 Mike and Ike candies
- small sharp knife

- 12 paper lollipop sticks
- toothpicks
- Styrofoam block
- prepared piping bag containing super white candy coating

PREPARATION:

Using a cookie scoop, scoop and shape cake pop dough into solid, enclosed horseshoes. Place on a wax paper–lined cookie sheet. Chill in the refrigerator for 10–15 minutes.

While the dough chills, melt the super white candy wafers in the microwave in a silicone bowl. Thin the consistency with paramount crystals if necessary and let rest at room temperature for at least 5 minutes before dipping.

With a small knife, cut the Mike and Ike candies in the center, crosswise at a slight diagonal.

DECORATING:

Remove the dough shapes from the refrigerator. Let rest at room temperature for a few minutes. Dip about ⅓ inch of one end of the lollipop stick into the candy coating and then insert stick into the bottom and middle.

Then attach the cut Mike and Ike candies (the thumbs) by applying candy coating on the cut surface and pressing the candy into place along the side of the cake pop. Be sure to position it where the thumb would be, about ⅓ of the way down from the top.

Once you've attached all the sticks and candy thumbs, refrigerate the cake pops for 2–3 minutes to help harden the candy coating.

When you're ready to dip, hold the cake pop stick vertically, with the cake pop upside down. Dip into super white candy coating. Submerge completely and pull out. Lightly wiggle to allow the excess coating to slide off the top. Use a toothpick to pierce any air bubbles stuck in the coating or to guide excess candy coating off of the cake pop. Turn right side up and place on a Styrofoam block to dry completely.

Advanced: Using a piping bag with melted super white candy coating, pipe vertical lines along the wrist area and pipe "V" shapes vertically aligned throughout the mitten. This creates a knitted look.

KRIS GALICIA BROWN

CANDY MINTS

You'll need:

- 12 uncoated cake balls shaped like round-edged discs, chilled
- wax paper
- cookie sheet
- 1 (16-oz.) bag super white candy wafers
- silicone bowl, or a deep microwave-safe plastic bowl or cup
- paramount crystals
- 12 paper lollipop sticks
- toothpicks
- Styrofoam block
- prepared piping bag containing red candy coating
- prepared piping bag containing green candy coating
- food-safe cellophane (optional)
- twist ties (optional)

PREPARATION:

Using a cookie scoop, scoop and shape cake pop dough into round-edged discs, like the shape of a giant M&M. Place on a wax paper–lined cookie sheet. Chill in the refrigerator for 10–15 minutes.

While the dough chills, melt the super white candy wafers in the microwave in a silicone bowl. Thin the consistency with paramount crystals if necessary and let rest at room temperature for at least 5 minutes before dipping.

DECORATING:

Remove the discs from the refrigerator. Let rest at room temperature for a few minutes. Dip about ⅓ inch of one end of the lollipop stick into the candy coating and then insert into the disc through the edge and into the middle.

Once you've attached all the sticks to the discs, you can refrigerate them for 2–3 minutes to help set the candy coating.

When you're ready to dip, hold the cake pop stick vertically, with the cake pop upside down. Dip into super white candy coating. Submerge completely and pull out. Lightly wiggle to allow the excess coating to slide off the top edge. Use a toothpick to pierce any air bubbles stuck in the coating or to guide excess candy coating off the cake pop. Turn right side up and place on a Styrofoam block.

Beginners: Using the red and green piping bags, pipe lines that radiate from the center out. If you're afraid of making a mistake or unsure of your piping skills, use a toothpick to etch out some guidelines on the coating and then trace those etchings when you pipe. Display your candy mints by wrapping them with food-safe cellophane and closing the ends with twist ties.

Advanced: Use the wet-on-wet technique (pg. 25) when piping your candy swirls!

KRIS GALICIA BROWN

candy mint

holiday tree

KRIS GALICIA BROWN

HOLIDAY TREES

You'll need:

- 12 uncoated cake balls shaped like cones, chilled
- wax paper
- cookie sheet
- 1 (16-oz.) bag green candy wafers

- silicone bowl, or a deep microwave-safe plastic bowl or cup
- paramount crystals
- 12 paper lollipop sticks
- toothpicks
- 12 jumbo star sprinkles

- white sugar pearls or mini confetti sprinkles
- prepared piping bag containing green candy coating
- Styrofoam block

PREPARATION:

Using a cookie scoop, scoop and shape cake pop dough into cones. Place on a wax paper–lined cookie sheet. Chill in the refrigerator for 10–15 minutes.

While the dough chills, melt green candy coating in the microwave in a silicone bowl. Thin the consistency with paramount crystals if necessary and let rest at room temperature for at least 5 minutes before dipping.

DECORATING:

Remove the cones from the refrigerator. Let rest at room temperature for a few minutes. Dip about ¼ inch of the end of lollipop stick into the candy coating and then insert stick into the circular base center of each cone.

Once you've attached all the sticks to the cones, refrigerate them for 2–3 minutes to help set the candy coating.

When you're ready to dip, hold the cake pop stick vertically, with the cake pop upside down. Dip into green candy coating. Submerge completely and pull out. Lightly wiggle to allow the excess coating to slide off the tip of the cone. Use a toothpick to pierce any air bubbles stuck in the coating or to guide excess coating off the cake pop. Turn tree right side up and, while the tip is still wet, add a star sprinkle to stand at the top. Place on a Styrofoam block to dry.

Beginners: Using a toothpick, dot green candy coating around the side of the tree in areas you want to add "ornaments." Attach sugar pearls or confetti sprinkles to those areas.

Advanced: Using a prepared piping bag with green candy coating, pipe coating on the lower ⅓ portion of the tree using quick up-and-down motions that form tight zigzags around the tree. Repeat for all the trees and let harden. Repeat the same motion in the middle ⅓ of the tree. This piping layer should overlap the top half of the piping you did previously. Let harden. Repeat with the top ⅓ of the tree.

Dot green candy coating in areas you want to add "ornaments" and then place sugar pearls or confetti sprinkles in those areas. Let dry completely.

KRIS GALICIA BROWN

Cake and Binder RECIPES

Here you'll find recipes for cakes and binders that I have fine-tuned for cake pop making. I've modified my favorite recipes so that you can easily achieve the perfect texture.

Cakes

The four basic recipes that follow are the exact recipes I use for my cake pops, and everyone should have them in their arsenal. These recipes are tried and tested and are some of my personal favorites. They yield a great texture to work with when making cake pop dough and forming shapes.

VANILLA BEAN CAKE

Ingredients:

- ¾ cup butter, room temperature
- 1¾ cups sugar
- 2 large eggs
- 2½ tsp. vanilla bean paste
- 2½ cups flour
- 2½ tsp. baking powder
- ½ tsp. salt
- ¾ cup milk
- ½ cup heavy cream

Preheat oven to 350°F.

In a large bowl, using a stand mixer with paddle attachment or a handheld mixer, cream together butter and sugar. Add the eggs one at a time until incorporated. Add vanilla bean paste.

Combine flour, baking powder, and salt in a medium-sized bowl. Add the flour mixture into the large bowl in three batches, adding the milk and then heavy cream between each batch of flour. Mix until combined between each addition. Scrape bowl as needed. Once all ingredients are combined, continue to beat on medium-high for 2 minutes.

Pour batter into a 9 × 13 baking pan and bake for 35 minutes or until cake tester comes out clean.

This recipe makes about 48 cake pop portions.

SNICKERDOODLE CAKE

Ingredients:

- 1 cup butter, room temperature
- 1¾ cups sugar
- 4 large eggs
- 2 tsp. pure vanilla extract
- 2¾ cups flour
- ¼ cup cornstarch
- 1 Tbsp. baking powder
- ½ tsp. salt
- 1 Tbsp. ground cinnamon
- 1¼ cups milk

Preheat oven to 350°F.

In a large bowl, using a stand mixer with the paddle attachment or a handheld mixer, cream together butter and sugar. Add the eggs one at a time until incorporated. Add vanilla.

In another bowl, whisk together all dry ingredients.

Add flour mixture to wet mixture in three batches, alternating with milk, starting and ending with flour. Continue to beat on medium-high for 2 minutes.

Pour batter into a 9 × 13 baking pan and bake for 40–45 minutes or until cake tester comes out clear.

This recipe makes about 70 cake pop portions.

CHOCOLATE CAKE

Ingredients:

- 1¾ cups flour
- 2 cups sugar
- ¾ cups unsweetened cocoa powder

- 2 tsp. baking soda
- 1 tsp. baking powder
- 1 tsp. salt
- 1 cup buttermilk

- ½ cup vegetable oil
- 2 large eggs
- 1 tsp. pure vanilla extract
- 1 cup boiling water

Preheat oven to 350°F.

In a large bowl, combine all dry ingredients with a whisk or, if using a stand mixer with the paddle attachment, combine dry ingredients using the lowest speed setting.

Slowly add buttermilk, oil, eggs, and vanilla to dry ingredients. When combined, add hot water and stir until just combined.

Pour batter into a 9 × 13 baking pan and bake for 40–45 minutes or until cake tester comes out clean.

This recipe makes about 56 cake pop portions.

KRIS GALICIA BROWN

RED VELVET CAKE

Ingredients:

½ cup shortening

1½ cups sugar

2 large eggs

1 Tbsp. red food coloring

3 Tbsp. unsweetened
  cocoa powder

1 tsp. pure vanilla extract

1 tsp. salt

2 cups flour

¼ cup cornstarch

1 cup buttermilk

1 tsp. baking soda

1 tsp. vinegar

Preheat oven to 350°F.

In a large bowl, using a stand mixer with paddle attachment or handheld mixer, cream shortening, sugar, and eggs. Add red food coloring, cocoa powder, vanilla, and salt to creamed mixture.

Combine flour and cornstarch. Add flour mixture to the mixture in the large bowl, alternating with buttermilk in three batches, starting and ending with the flour mixture.

Add soda to vinegar and blend into cake batter. Continue to beat on medium-high for 2 minutes. Don't be alarmed—the batter color will not look like a true red. After baking, crumbling, adding a binder, and compressing to make cake pop dough, trust me, you'll have the perfect shade of red.

Pour batter into a 9 × 13 baking pan and bake for 35–40 minutes or until cake tester comes out clean.

This recipe makes about 44 cake pop portions.

Binders

A binder is what you mix into the crumbled cake that helps to bind everything together to form cake pop dough. Frosting or buttercream is typically used, but there are other options.

Since such a small quantity of binder is used, taste is not a huge factor. I usually use my homemade cream cheese or honey buttercream for any cake flavor. They're both thick and creamy—perfect for cake pop making. For beginners, store-bought frosting is an excellent option, but make sure you purchase the rich and creamy–style frosting.

A healthier option is plain ol' cream cheese. Trust me, it goes well with every flavor. Caramel and ganache are also other options, but I still prefer and recommend my cream cheese or honey buttercream, plain cream cheese, or store-bought rich and creamy–style frosting.

KRIS GALICIA BROWN

CREAM CHEESE BUTTERCREAM

Ingredients:

- ¾ cup butter, room temperature
- 1 (8-oz.) pkg. cream cheese, slightly softened
- 2 cups powdered sugar, sifted

Using a hand mixer or stand mixer, beat butter and cream cheese at medium speed until combined and creamy. Add powdered sugar ½ cup at a time on low speed until combined. Beat at medium speed for 1 minute.

This recipe makes 3 cups. Refrigerate unused buttercream in an airtight container for up to 3 days, or freeze in ¼-cup or ½-cup portions wrapped in two layers of plastic wrap and sealed in a small labeled and dated freezer bag. If freezing, thaw in the refrigerator prior to use.

HONEY BUTTERCREAM

Ingredients:

- ½ cup butter, room temperature
- 2 cups powdered sugar
- ⅓ cup honey*

Using a hand mixer or stand mixer, beat butter at medium speed until creamy. Add powdered sugar ½ cup at a time on low speed until combined.

Add honey and beat at medium speed for 1 minute.

This recipe makes 1½ cups. Refrigerate unused buttercream in an airtight container for up to 2 weeks, or freeze in ¼-cup or ½-cup portions wrapped in two layers of plastic wrap and sealed in a small labeled and dated freezer bag. If freezing, thaw in the refrigerator and remix if necessary prior to use.

Please note and take into consideration that honey is to be avoided for all children under 1 year old. Substitute ⅓ cup light corn syrup for honey if necessary.

KRIS GALICIA BROWN

Cake and Candy Supplies

I urge you to support and buy from local businesses as much as you possibly can. Google "cake and candy supplies" and search within your area to see what's available. Craft stores and certain retail stores should also carry some cake and candy making materials. Here is a list of online sources that carry all the basic supplies as well as my preferred Merckens or Clasen candy coating brand:

COUNTRY KITCHEN SWEETART
www.shopcountrykitchen.com

CK PRODUCTS
www.ckproducts.com

STANDLEE'S
www.standlees.com

CANDYLAND CRAFTS
www.candylandcrafts.com

STREICHS
www.streichs.com

LINNEA'S (WHOLESALE ONLY)
www.linneasinc.com

Here are some retail chain craft stores that also carry the basics you'll need and may have a location near you:

MICHAELS
www.michaels.com

HOBBY LOBBY
www.hobbylobby.com

JO-ANN
www.joann.com

A.C. MOORE
www.acmoore.com

CANDIES AND SPRINKLES

Here's a little secret: Drug stores and party supply stores are a gold mine for candies. Drug stores carry certain novelty candies year-round, like candy corn, jelly beans, and candy necklaces. Certain chains of grocery stores carry different candies as well.

Here are also a few online sources I recommend for candy and sprinkles in addition to the ones listed above:

GLOBAL SUGAR ART
www.globalsugarart.com

CANDY WAREHOUSE
www.candywarehouse.com

OH! NUTS (KOSHER)
www.ohnuts.com

PARTY CITY
www.partycity.com

SAVE ON CRAFTS
www.save-on-crafts.com

SILICONE BOWLS

Available at: www.amazon.com

My most favorite bowls are iSi 1-cup silicone prep bowls with lids (set of 3). They are available on Amazon.

MINI BUTTON CHOCOLATE MOLD

Available at: www.shopcountrykitchen.com • www.ckproducts.com

Product #90-13709.

PAPER STRAWS

Available at: www.greenpartygoods.com

These straws are available in an array of colors and designs. They are from Green Party Goods, which offers much more than awesome vibrant paper straws!

KRIS GALICIA BROWN

CAKE POP STANDS

Available at: www.kcbakes.com

I love and highly recommend the wood cake pop stands made by KC Bakes. They are high quality and come in a variety of sizes and designs too! I like to cover the cake pop stands in wrapping paper to match any party or event theme. I also wrap my stands in plastic wrap and use them for everyday cake pop making instead of Styrofoam blocks. And the plastic wrap makes for an easy cleanup!

KRIS GALICIA BROWN

Index

INDEX

Chris Wojdak Photography

ABOUT THE AUTHOR

About the Author

With a love for sweets and a passion for design, Kris Galicia Brown is a light of inspiration in the cake pop industry. Kris skillfully crafts her sweets like works of fine art.

After graduating with a degree in advertising from the Art Institute of California–San Diego, she pursued a career in graphic design and worked as lead creative for an advertising and PR agency. After entering motherhood, Kris founded kCreative and began work as a freelance designer and ultimately stumbled upon the world of cake pops. Her background as a graphic designer has proved to be an excellent foundation for her newest venture.

Kris's originality, eye for detail, and addiction to precision sets her apart from other cake pop makers and has landed her on top of a global audience. In addition to running her business, Goods by kCreative, she also teaches cake pop classes and blogs regularly. Kris lives in San Diego, California, with her husband and two daughters.

Learn more about Kris Galicia Brown at
www.goodsbykcreative.com
www.facebook.com/kcreativecakepops